ON ROUTE
the art of carnival

Edited by Pax Nindi

ARTS COUNCIL ENGLAND

Published jointly by The X Press and Arts Council England

The X Press
PO Box 25694
London N17 6FP
Tel: 020 8801 2100
Fax: 020 8885 1322
E-mail: vibes@xpress.co.uk
Web site: www.xpress.co.uk

Arts Council England
14 Great Peter Street
London SW1P 3NQ
Tel: 0870 300 6200
Textphone: 020 7973 6564
Web site: www.artscouncil.org.uk

Charity registration no. 1036733

To order this book through Arts Council England, or to download it, see www.artscouncil.org.uk

Designed by **k3 & kargan media**
Tel: 07960 987294
E-mail: info@k3media.demon.co.uk

Printed by
Favil Press
127 South Street
Lancing
West Sussex
BN15 8AS

Distributed in UK by **Turnaround Distribution**
Unit 3, Olympia Trading Estate, Coburg Road, London N22 6TZ
Tel: 020 8829 3000
Fax: 020 8881 5088

ISBN 1-874509-82-4

Contents

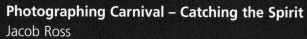
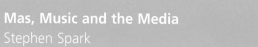

Preface

On Route and its writers demonstrate the ever-evolving characteristic of carnival arts and its contribution to British contemporary arts and culture. In order to maintain the true carnival ambience the authors have been encouraged to write in ways that they feel comfortable with.

As we have included some carnival issues that have never been written about before I hope the book is going to increase your understanding of the world's greatest art form. Considering the unlimited subjects carnival offers for debate, we are confident that this book will encourage the public, artists, writers and the media to take the art form seriously.

Although the On Route chapters are mainly on Caribbean style carnivals we have included other carnival forms. There are so many exciting carnival developments taking place in this country that it is impossible to include them all in one book. Our hope is that On Route will act as a catalyst for future carnival publications. Recent developments include; carnival theatre, the Queen's Golden Jubilee, soca aerobics, international fellowships, new technology as well as carnival processions taking place in non-traditional carnival venues such as Glastonbury Festival and the Royal Opera House.

Over the past few years, the growth of carnival arts has led to international collaborations and commissions allowing artists to travel around the globe more than ever. It is inspiring to know that public institutions and authorities are working with carnivalists to deliver carnival events and that in schools artists are contributing to the curriculum, allowing some carnivalists to work all year round.

Gone are the days when the aesthetics and artistic practices carnival arts represented were underdeveloped, misunderstood and unknown in England and abroad. Various individuals, artists and organisations contribute endless hours to preparing for carnivals throughout the country. It is important to acknowledge those artists and individuals who, despite all the carnival politics and lack of proper financial support, make the art form what it is today.

On Route has been developed over three years and every effort has been made to contact authors and photographers of material published within it. We would be glad to hear from unacknowledged sources at the first opportunity.

Pax Nindi
Senior Carnival Officer
Arts Council England

Foreword

Crossing cultures and spanning generations, Carnival is at the heart of community cultural activity in towns, villages and cities throughout Britain.

On Route is a wonderful guide to the diverse experience of carnival in the UK. While focussing on African Caribbean style carnival arts, it provides a snapshot and flavour of carnival as it develops and grows across our country.

It has not been possible for this book to cover all the positive contributions that are being made by carnivals to the cultural, economic and social development of our communities. However, it is the first in a series of exciting initiatives that seek to explore and promote a better understanding of carnival arts activities.

The government continues to recognise carnival's contribution to cultural heritage and with Arts Council England has invested in the future of carnival. On Route provides a glimpse into carnival's past and celebrates the contribution that carnival can make to our future.

Tessa Blackstone

Rt Hon Baroness Tessa Blackstone
Minister for the Arts

Serious Business

Dotun
Adebayo

t's 96°F in the shade. Real hot, but nobody seems to mind. This is Leeds and it's jollification time with a breathtaking kaleidoscope of colour, music and sheer spectacle.

Dotun Adebayo

is an outspoken columnist whose work appears in many magazines and national newspapers. He hosts his own show on BBC radio and has written several books including "Can I Have My Balls Back" and "Promised Land".

Come Monday, things will get even hotter, but this is Carnival Saturday and the judging of the carnival queen and calypso monarch competitions. After fighting off some stiff competition in amazing costumes, eighteen-year-old Stacey Morris is crowned carnival queen. Stacey is a second-generation carnival queen. Her mother was a previous carnival queen of Leeds and was twice crowned carnival queen of Leicester. Stacey herself won the title in Leicester three months previously with a magnificent costume depicting 'Under the Witches hat', to go with the carnival theme of 'Magical Fantasy'. The costume, a huge black pointed witch's hat, covered her entire body. When a lever was pulled the hat elevated seventeen feet above her head to reveal a colourful costume and the huge face of a laughing hyena. The face was made up of 5,500 sequins which Stacey had hand-stapled herself and silks, satins and glitter adding the final touch. Serious business!

Carnival is serious business, and not just to carnival queens. Leeds attracts calypsonians, steelbands and sound systems from all over the country and crowds from all over the world come to savour its particular brand of carnival, if not its bazaar of colourful stalls selling jerk chicken, goat curry, sugar cane, barbecue corn, chilli and rice and anything else you can think of.

To have the two biggest carnivals clashing on the same day is an option no one should have to choose between. Alas, that is the choice that is made every August Bank Holiday Monday between attending Notting Hill and Leeds. It's not as simple as a North/South divide.

Notting Hill Carnival has become a major tourist attraction and has accommodated all cultures. In Europe it is now dubbed as Europe's biggest street event with an ability to attract over two million people in two days.

Leeds, on the other hand, has taken its lead from Trinidad and prided and billed itself as the traditional West Indian carnival. Despite attracting large crowds, sound systems are not allowed to take over the Carnival with high decibels, not whilst there is a large community in the city from St. Kitts and Trinidad to prevent it and ensure that the Carnival stays 'traditional'. And even though sound systems line the streets on route, only traditional instruments are allowed on the three hour procession itself as it snakes its way through Chapeltown and back to Potternewton Park.

Sunday's big reggae concert attracts huge stars, but it is the official opening of the Carnival on Sunday night, 'Jour ouvert', that makes Leeds so special. No other carnival in Britain is officially opened in the middle of the night with music and dancing in the streets, lanes and parks until morning. After the Monday parade the event culminates with a last lap dance of the marquee to a calypso band until 4am.

In nearby Manchester, where Carnival FM has been promoting the carnival, the Caribbean community has not responded well to the invitation to turn their carnival parade into a Caribbean affair. Not surprising that it has being renamed Manchester International Caribbean Carnival! Even though there are a few steel bands on the procession, it could just as easily be the Lord Mayor's Parade.

At dusk, the carnival dies down, but the revelry moves on to the local clubs late into the night. One can't help thinking that if Manchester had a larger Trinidadian population, its Carnival might also be more 'traditional'. But having a large Trinidadian community of its own is not sufficient to make a successful carnival. The right mix of street procession and party is needed.

For Carnival no longer comes just once a year, far from it. In Britain alone it comes at least twenty times and maybe more. For all around the country, every city of note has its own carnival, and many small towns too - Leeds, Huddersfield, Liverpool, Manchester, Preston, Bradford, Leicester, Nottingham and Derby for example. And every carnival has its own special atmosphere.

Back in the day, carnival was synonymous with Notting Hill and loosely based on the model brought over by Trinidadian immigrants. Notting Hill Carnival had the history, the costumes, the music and the people. It also had the setting: in a somewhat anarchic about turn, the local council allowed revellers to take over the streets of Notting Hill, Ladbroke Grove and Westbourne Park for a seemingly hedonistic overflow of joy and happiness. Notting Hill also had a mix of tradition and modernity that seemed to work. For the traditionalists there

was the masquerade bands, decorated floats, calypsonians, mobile soca sounds and steelbands. For the modernists, the static sound systems playing reggae, hip hop, hardcore, soul, swing, jungle, funk, Brazilian and African music.

My carnival journey through Britain started in late May, Spring Bank Holiday, when I joined 100,000 other smiling faces at the Luton International Carnival, a multi-cultural affair with the town's Asian, English, Irish and Caribbean communities all represented on the fourteen sound stages around Luton displaying their own carnival traditions to celebrate everything from nature, harvest and fertilisation to the struggle for freedom and expression.

Four square miles of Luton town centre is shut off to traffic from 8am to 8pm in order to parade the spectacular costumes that had been created over the previous two months at the Luton mas-camp. Yet it still takes three hours for the mile long procession of 2,000 participants (amongst them local nurses and firemen, thirty decorated floats including the St. Kitts, Nevis and Friends Association's Ancient Egyptian theme, and a hundred steel drums beating out a non-stop rhythm) to leave Warden Park and cover the four mile route - and even longer for the Moko Jumbie stilt troupe.

Derby also takes place mostly in a park, the local Osmaston Park, which it shares with a fun fair for its mix of entertainment by sound systems and live performers including pop and reggae stars. The day before the carnival, however, a small procession makes its way through the city centre to Market Place for a street party featuring live performances from gospel choirs, steel bands and dancers followed by a carnival dance in the evening.

Lest you should forget that the Leicester Carnival has its background in history and culture, it takes place on the first Saturday of August to coincide with the emancipation from slavery. I followed the mas bands and steel bands on their procession from Victoria Park, and by the time you arrive back a Victoria Park two miles from the city centre, 120,000 people from all over the Midlands await you.

If you arrive in Leicester on carnival day, you'll miss out on Culture Week that precedes it with a taster of what is to come: local poets, steel bands, dancers etc. The Carnival Queen Show itself takes place seven days before, attracting a local audience of up to 3000 locals at De Montfort Hall, who will cheer the victorious lady on to representing Leicester at the subsequent Rotterdam carnival.

Some people go to carnival for the music, some people go for the 'vibes'. Or to bump into people they haven't seen all year and make up some new acquaintances. Some people go to taste the home cooking on offer from the hundreds of mobile kitchens - lessons in the different ways to cook Caribbean food. Some people go for panorama - the steel band competition that takes place the day before the Notting Hill Carnival. Others go to party on the streets, to identify with and take part in the street parades and understand the traditions and culture surrounding them, or simply to jump up or enjoy barbers competing for the battle of the barbers. Where else can you enter and choose your spot and get this much entertainment for free? Where else can you dress up in fancy costume and run through the streets dancing with your music turned up?

But this is no easy-come-by freeness. These people have been working all year round to achieve the right mix of music, costume, art, history and flavour, the mas players painstakingly stitching and weaving feathers and gold bands into their creative costumes while the steel bands endlessly harmonise in the pan yards. But be that as it may, all I can say is 'Praise Be' for all the good times I've had at carnivals up and down the country. ■

Lloyd Blake Birmingham Carnival

One particular year, I was asked if we could help the children at a nursery in Handsworth. They were waiting for a carnival float that didn't show up. We did manage to get a float out to them so they could take part in the Carnival. It was very emotional for us as we watched the "Thank you", coming out of their mouths at the end of the day. Also the teachers, the look on their faces, knowing they would have been devastated if the children had been let down. Things like that touch you and stay with you.

To Carnival is to Join In!

[Grenada, 1953]

Joan
Anim-Addo

My own memories associate Carnival with town.
Social satire and double speak was the language of road
marches and king and queen parades at Queens Park,
the local multi-purpose stadium of some repute.

Joan Anim-Addo
was born in Grenada.
She is currently Head of the
Caribbean Centre and
lecturer within the English
Department at Goldsmiths
College, University of London.
She is Chair of the Caribbean
Women Writers Alliance (CWWA)
and founder-editor of
Mango Season, the journal on
Caribbean Women's writing.
Joan's published writing includes
poetry, fiction, drama and history
as well as critical writing.

Carnival day arrives. Our clothes are laid out, ready on the bed. Skirts are of three primary colours: red green and yellow. We've helped (though my mother possibly viewed the process differently) with the making of the skirts. We've drawn the threads for ample gathers for each of the three tiers. We've assisted with the pinning of bands of zig-zag braid on each seam separating the colours. We've helped manoeuvre the treadle as my mother guided the fabric under the eye of the sewing machine. My sister was too young, so my story goes. The Carnival clothes are ready. My sister's cut-away-at-the-shoulder top is green; mine is red. Matching ribbons already make large floppy butterfly bows around our plaits. We're going to Carnival.

Carnival? I wondered lately:
verb or noun?
"We go carnival today"!
So, verb of colour; doing word.
taking an active part -
make yu clothes
get in yu band
or, join a passin one
for all o we have favourite.
See hips big and small
Catch de calypso rhythm.
Let your own move free
work up a hot hot thirst
and take a swig,
wet your throat;
slake desire a moment.
Meantime mas band for so!
To carnival is to join in!

We joined in. This much everyone knew of Carnival.

At the edge of the town, bands begin to appear. Steel pans massed in rows move with the tide of black and brown bodies along the main road. The throng of people fall away to the grassy edge or concrete sidewalk. Costumed figures in the band hold their privileged position directly behind the pan men. They sing and twirl, gyrate, execute fancy steps, forwards, sideways, backwards. Yes, backwards even,

when the band is forced to wait, blocked by mas bands and crowds ahead. I have later known many a veteran carnival reveller confess that throughout the days of playing mas she dared not stop; dared not sit down for fear that her knees would lock and she'd never get up again. So, the masqueraders dance on relentlessly. Sleep will come days later. Meantime relief stays at hand courtesy of water bottle, hip flask or something similar.

... metal clinking on metal
jhab jhab
metal clinking on metal
jhab jhab
I want a penny
jhab jhab
give me a penny
jhab jhab
to pay my passage
jhab jhab
to go back to hell
jhab jhab...

We younger children fled furthest away from the front of the house and the metallic "jhab jhab" refrain. My earliest memory of flight from this sound and the fearful image it conjured up takes me to the crouched figure of a child hiding way, way under the bed, as near to the wall as possible and away from any revealing source of light. But as I recall, I never quite held out. I heard the voices calling; heeded them. I would creep to the veranda and, holding on to my grandmother's rocking chair, peer down through the wooden slats of floorboards.

Downstairs, a knot of adults are gathered. Among them, stands the figure of dread. My grandmother beckons to me. We walk quietly

down the back stairs. An adult voice says laughing, "All yu children give the jhab jhab a penny yet? Or you want him to stay all day?"

My grandmother slips a penny into my palm. I peep through the crack formed by the open door. The jhab jhab, a raggedy near naked figure, blackened and greasy, with hair matted and blood red lips stands among the uncles. An oily chain hangs from the jhab jhabs' neck. It scrapes along the concrete flooring as he moves. Despite my grandmother's urging I will go no nearer. Rather, I retreat indoors and hand the penny only from the safety of the window on to the veranda. A faint smell of overproof rum and mechanic's oil blows indoors with the breeze from the veranda.

jhab jhab
I want a penny
jhab jhab
to pay my passage
jhab jhab
to go back to hell

His fingers encased in thin cylinders of recycled tin play out the rhythm and a sparse procession begins to gather in the red gravely road. Young children hug nearby trees or tug at mothers' skirts. The more knowing, especially the boys laugh as they jostle each other. A second jhab jhab appears from the direction of my aunt's house. He flails the air with a long whip he is carrying; he secures the chain being dragged in the gravel. His partner, the first jhab jhab stands quivering. Both the chain and the whip bind them. Together they act out a mime in which force, terror and torture dominate. Darkness and the whip appear central

to this. Finally, the refrain sounds. The jhab jhabs call, voices respond and an insistent beat echoes through the late mornings island heat. Gradually voices grow faint along with the disappearing jhab jhab figures but the clanking continues to ring through tropical hills only growing steadily more faint.

Shatnees. Silence masked.
Memory in mask, mirrors and talc.
So, history turn ole mas
to teach its lesson
and though now the dust seems white
once not so long ago, blood red
caked black skin.
So, the whip still lives
for us dirt stained ones;
us cow whipped children of dust
though sweat, like fear wears a different perfume.

We may call it 'talc'. No matter.
We, Anansi's children can, at least
sniff a trick by now.
Oh we should know
- who else - how the taste of it
lies silent, curdled on the tongue
patient while memory piggybacks
or gags on the ole Adams' apple
waiting as we learn again
the gift of speech.

My first and most enduring history lessons came from Carnival. Bands of Caribs passed year after year before my eyes. The whitened figures of the Conquistadors, both foreign and strangely familiar, puzzled me. The jhab jhab I searched out warily. Watched for their small bands of three or so. All was wonder. What meant most were the 'Tim Tim' figures of the oral tradition I knew so well. I marvelled that the Lajablesse woman of one goat foot and one human one, she who should so be feared by men, swayed gently as she walked the streets of St.George's. That she was beautiful in her low cut shiny taffeta dress glistening in the sunlight did not surprise me. Nothing surprised; much aroused wonder. The fiery Ligarous in hoops of flame showed no sign of fear in the daylight, though every child knew they should be transformed back into human disguise by daybreak. Or else... And there's Mr. Anansi looking smarter than I could possibly have imagined him. But then, he too would have known he was visiting town!

My mother asks if we're ready to go home. She is teasing; she knows we are not. I still want to catch my favourites, the 'shatnees' (short knees) or as my grandmother refers to them, "de ole time masqueraders". There is nothing stunning about the shatnees in the way that some carnival bands can be stunning. Their pink gauze like masks mesmerise but the surround of the masks, the frame of fabric like my grandmother's madras head-ties make for certain resonances I do not at the time comprehend. The shatnees slip in and out of the crowd, agile on their washiconged (like sneakers) feet. They sprinkle talcum powder randomly as they jump up in the streets. The mirrors on their costume reflect back the light, twinkling at us children. Unlike the jhab jhabs who seemed too much like giants, the 'shatnees' were of average height. Unlike the jhab jhab, the shatnees were silent.

Older, I would join young adults seeking out J'ouvert morning where the spirit of ole time carnival lives and obstinately refuses the harsh glare of day. I would discover the stick fighters, jhab jhabs a plenty, shatnees too, but also something elusive, a greater sense of an earlier, darker period when revellers walked out 'fore day mornin' because the day was not your own. Individuals pass before you with their bodies painted. There are people dressed in old clothes, some half-naked. The large bands which rely on showmanship and daylight are absent but there is a kind of witnessing, singly or in twos and threes in the pre-dawn of J'ouvert morning.

On the streets of London I find something else though, of course, never J'ouvert. History? Yes; lots. Adaptation? Yes. Carnival? A London dub festival version. I see Eastern Caribbean culture framed in the eyes of many others. I see hybridity, gyration, sound systems, sex. These perceptions could conceivably be just about growing up but I doubt it. More importantly, I look for the shatnees and I am relieved to find them, fragments of memory still held in their mirrors. And the jhab jhabs too hold true to tradition. Even the whip has reappeared. Such continuity takes us, of course, well beyond recent memory. And in the time between? Cracks have begun to appear in the collective silence. The meaning of the jhab jhab insists upon being articulated in newly written histories, there as well as here where we have travelled and where so many have stayed. Meantime, a new generation gaze wide eyed on figures from the past, on mask, mirror, talc and upon much more besides; a resilient culture establishing itself on the streets of Britain regardless. ▪

School Mas'
– Catching Them Young

Celia
Burgess-Macey

Imagine a hot summer afternoon...

Celia Burgess-Macey

is a Lecturer in Primary and
Early Years Education at
Goldsmiths College,
University of London. She has
been involved in carnival as a
teacher, teacher educator
and carnivalist for almost 20
years and has been
developing carnival in the
curriculum in London primary
schools. She is a member of
Yaa Asantewaa mas band.

In the school playground parents and toddlers are milling around. The steel band from the local secondary school is setting up at one end of the playground under the shade of a tree. Today they will be playing for a real audience. There is an atmosphere of festivity and anticipation. It's carnival at a south London primary school. The weeks of hard work, in which children have learnt about carnival and carnival arts and have planned, made, and are now about to wear, their carnival costumes are about to bear fruit. The head-teacher appears to thank everyone for coming. He is dressed up for the occasion wearing a large hat representing his head teacher role. It is in the shape of a desk piled high with recent Government curriculum initiatives! But today he is not behind his desk. He is inviting everyone to "Jump up, play Mas' and enjoy carnival."

The parade begins. Each class has chosen a separate theme. The youngest children are in costumes as flowers. My mind flashes back to St. Crispin's Primary school in Port of Spain, Trinidad where I first witnessed a school's carnival. The nursery children there were also flowers in practically identical form to these. In general, classes have linked their costume theme to a topic or area of the curriculum that they are studying, or to stories that they have been reading together. Long-necked giraffes and large-eared elephants appear; this class is representing the animals of Africa. The teacher is the lion. A mathematical theme is represented by a class dressed as dominoes. A group of delighted and fierce looking girls appear inside a pirate boat costume gleefully waving their swords. Not for them the passive maiden waiting to be rescued! My own favourite costumes today are those of the year 2 class depicting characters from the poetry of Edward Lear. This class is being taught by a Goldsmith's College teacher-trainee student and she has taken an imaginative leap to use the texts being studied by the children in the literacy hour as the inspiration for carnival costumes. The 'man with the very long beard' is a particularly amusing creation.

Teachers in other schools have made similar creative use of the statutory Programmes of Study of the National Curriculum. I have seen costumes representing the weather and the ubiquitous topic on ancient Egypt has stimulated the production of costumes representing Egyptian gods, pharaohs and sphinxes. In this respect, school carnival is very like both Notting Hill and Trinidad Carnivals where black history themes are often taken to inspire beautiful recreations.

It is an axiom of carnival that any theme, however abstract the idea may be, can result in an imaginative representation in a carnival band. In one school tie-dye materials made costumes representing watery colour themes for 'Under The Sea' and in another brightly coloured feathers of parrots. Environmental awareness studies were exemplified in "Our Green World" with each class taking a different

aspect. Children working on animal and bird masks learnt wire bending techniques to create large scale headpiece costumes of animals linked to the study of the Anansi stories. Food technology was studied through the making of Caribbean dishes, especially food that can be carried on carnival day.

More and more schools in England are incorporating aspects of carnival studies into the curriculum or taking part in local carnivals such as those that take place each year in Hackney, Lambeth, Luton, Watford, Huddersfield, Nottingham, Birmingham and Reading and in many other cities, towns and boroughs. In a sense this is not new as schools in Trinidad and Tobago regularly incorporate carnival and many compete nationally in the schools' carnival parade on the Saturday before Carnival proper. Also schools in Cuba, Portugal and Spain take part in schools' carnival parades. Although the current development of carnivals in schools here is a direct response to the Caribbean carnival started in Notting Hill, schools often incorporate other elements dating back to the old fairs, feast days and carnivals in this country. In these carnivals, costumed fools and clowns performed and mocked at their rulers.

Carnival has always been a festival of the people. It has always responded and changed, incorporating different influences. Carnival as it is celebrated in Britain today has its historical roots in Caribbean carnival, which itself has brought together African, Amerindian, Asian and European cultural forms. It is also crucially rooted in the historic struggles for liberation by enslaved African peoples. It is important for children studying carnival to be aware of these more serious political and historical dimensions; to learn that black people were forbidden to play their own music and that the African drum was banned at many points during the colonial period. This is what led to the invention of the steel pan. The slaves were forbidden to hold many of their traditional festivals and the ending of slavery was celebrated with a carnival on the streets with music and dancing. It is also important to learn that the roots of Notting Hill Carnival are part of the struggle of African Caribbean peoples in this country against racism and oppression. The first London carnival celebration, held indoors in the winter, was a direct response to the 1958 race riots and the racist murder of Kelso Cochrane by white youths in 1959. The Notting Hill Carnival is then an assertion of black pride and black presence in this country. It is a statement of the right of minority communities to celebrate and contribute their cultures. It states "we are here to stay".

Of course the carnival celebration in the school described above is just the end of a process of curriculum development over a term or even longer. Carnival in a school has to be a collaborative, whole school effort and therefore planning has to begin some months before. It is normal in any case to plan projects long term in order that teachers can decide which aspects of the programmes of study of the subjects in the National Curriculum they will be able to cover. Schools also need time to contact local carnival organisations and carnival artists to organise specialist workshops. In many schools, both teachers and children have benefited from presentations or workshops on carnival costume design and mask making, the music of carnival (especially calypso and steel band), carnival dance rhythms and forms, poems and literary texts linked to carnival.

Carnival lends itself to a cross curricula approach and in different schools I have seen elements of most subjects being covered. There are obvious and immediate links to the programmes of study for art, music and dance as well as design and technology, but through their use of texts - poems, stories and songs linked to carnival, teachers have covered much of the English curriculum. Many schools invite storytellers from the black community linking this to 'Literacy hour'. In the buying and measuring of material and in studying pattern and symmetry there is much practical mathematics. In studying the origins of carnival and its current spread throughout the world, children could link carnival to the study of a distant environment as well as studying the reasons for the movements of people between countries and continents, including the movements within children's own families. So they will be studying both geography and history. Children have bent cane or wire, tie-dyed material, made papier mache, learnt wax resist techniques and batik, created structures which balance and move in particular ways, investigated science. Children may invent their own calypsos providing them with an opportunity to exercise humour and imagination as well as musical appreciation. In dance workshops they might explore bird movements. It must also be remembered that Carnival has its links to religious festivals being associated with Lent, so it can be tackled in the Religious Education curriculum.

Pupils in one school were impressed by an illustrated talk given by a secondary school student who talked about his and his family's involvement in playing 'mas' since he was six years old. He demonstrated his growing confidence, commitment and expertise as a performer, designer and member of his community carnival group. This opened up important considerations for teachers about the wider curriculum of values, of personal and social education and citizenship.

The statutory orders for national curriculum foundation subjects (including music, art, dance, design technology) were amended to allow schools to concentrate on the implementation of the literacy and numeracy strategies. This worried teachers and those concerned with arts education, and has led to a narrowing of children's experiences in the arts in many primary schools. However, a revised and slimmed down national curriculum was implemented from September 2000 and contains more references to cultural diversity and a clearer statement about the role of the arts in children's lives: "Art and design stimulates creativity and imagination. Understanding appreciation and enjoyment of visual arts have the power to enrich our personal and public lives." [Q.C.A. DfEE 2000]

Furthermore, the recent introduction of guidelines on citizenship in the curriculum can also be supportive to work on children's cultural identity and respect for diverse community traditions. Hollis Liverpool, otherwise known as "The Mighty Chalkdust", who is both teacher and calypsonian in Trinidad, puts it like this:

"If we are to produce citizens who will respond adequately to the challenges of the third world in general, Trinidad and Tobago in particular, the arts and culture must not be simply forms of life to indulge in for a while, basking in their glory merely for entertainment and then be heard no more but these forms must penetrate the school system, pierce our educators hearts and spread their tentacles through all the realms of learning so that we shall realise our aims. All aspects of our cultural life must be in our curriculum. We must aim at educating the whole personality and not lay the emphasis on the so called academic subjects, as if art and artforms are not academic or have academic value. Through our artforms we can make our education relevant".

There are therefore, powerful reasons why carnival is important in schools beyond implementing the National Curriculum. These reasons have more to do with some basic principles underlying children's learning. The development of children's creativity, building on their own ideas, the development of collaborative skills, the development of independence and resourcefulness and the ability to explore their ideas in practical and meaningful contexts with a very real end product in mind. These are all features of successful learning and carnival. Many teachers have commented that children who are often least motivated and unable to concentrate in school, and who may not be seen as high achievers, have surprised both their teachers and themselves by their enthusiastic involvement in carnival arts. Their sense of achievement through this work has been particularly great. This is not just true in British schools, but also applies to work on carnival in Trinidadian schools. The following quote taken from an interview with a teacher in Trinidad illustrates this point

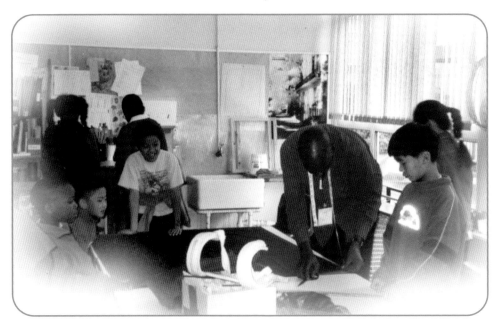

"The interest generated in the children in creating their 'mas' gives them a sense of their own development. Unless someone has the will you cannot teach them much but now they want to stay behind after school to work on their 'mas'. We reach some children who we have not touched in the year. They are children I will try my best to get something across to and they are just not interested. But now they have the feeling of the 'Mas'. They come up and say, 'I have an idea I want to make it like this. I want to draw it like this'. Then they will work on something that will represent their idea so that they can get it into the band. After they have participated in carnival they often have increased enthusiasm for their school life and most of the activities we have in carnival are oriented around their class work as we usually take a theme from their subject and help develop it. Of course as teachers we help the children choose what they want to do but we don't tell them. We bring in ideas. We teach them skills. We provide materials. We use a lot of local and recycled materials, but it is the children's work in the end".

Many teachers in schools have talked about this sudden flowering of achievement evidenced in children's work through carnival.

The process of opening out the curriculum to the wider community is the most important gain for schools of developing work on carnival. A growing number of carnival artists, in steel band, calypso, dance, costume creation and fabric design, are willing to work with schools. They have considerable skills of working with children, alongside teachers and communicating their art form in ways that are accessible to young children. The benefits to teachers of working with artists from the black community are also considerable as teachers learn new approaches, new ideas and themselves are able to broaden their experience and understanding of carnival and learn practical skills associated with carnival art forms. Of course, in all schools, whether they have children from African Caribbean communities or not, it is of tremendous value for children to see black adults in positions of authority and responsibility. This is particularly valuable where children see their own teachers also learning from these same black adults and working alongside them. This is a point made by John Egglestone in his pamphlet 'Arts Education in a multicultural society'.

"the artists played a key role far beyond that which they or anyone would normally have expected of artists. The curricula dimensions were created at the interface of understanding and communication between black and white participants. The influence on teachers' attitudes and thinking has also been powerful - not only have they discovered a way to enhance the curriculum, but also a way to challenge both manifest and latent racism in a new and effective way".

Of course this costs money. Some schools have had support from their Local Education Authority, from their local Arts Board or from other sources of funding, such as money raised by parents, and have been able to employ a number of artists over a period of time. I think it has been helpful for schools to have seen the development of carnival as a long term project, where they have been willing to experiment and to extend the range of artists they invite in to work with children over a number of years. This will mean that teachers within the school, parents of children in the school who may be involved through carnival, as well as people in the wider community, gradually build up their expertise and develop ways of working together. In some communities there will be local carnival groups, steel bands, 'mas' camps who will be a source of expertise, in other cases artists will need to be contacted through an Arts Council of England or internet source.

The response to and involvement of parents in carnival projects in schools has been good. Parents can help make costumes or contribute to thinking up themes and designs. One teacher describes the impact of the carnival project at her school as follows.

"Many of our black parents express concern over negative attitudes to Africa from their children and white people. The project enabled the school to give black culture a focus and to emphasise the African connection with the Caribbean and carnival. It has encouraged debate with parents and governors on the importance of a high visibility of black cultures".

Many parents and members of the extended family of children of Caribbean origin travel regularly to the Caribbean often bringing back pictures, stories of carnival, or the latest calypso records and newspapers. These could provide a valuable resource pool for teachers - rarely drawn on by schools. There are also an increasing number of web sites giving information on carnival bands, steel bands and carnivals around the world e.g. www.carnivalnet.org.uk. Carnival is rapidly becoming an important international event. Teachers from Lambeth schools that have been involved in carnival have produced an extensive and useful resource pack, including many colour illustrations, curriculum map, classroom activities and background information.

So what does a school need to do to develop carnival in their curriculum?

1. One committed person with some knowledge of carnival.

2. A willingness to learn and experiment on the part of several adults in the school.

3. The support of the head teacher and some commitment from school resources.

4. Input from outside the school from experienced carnivalists / carnival artists - these can be contacted through the Arts Council or local Arts Boards.

5. A commitment to inform and involve parents and governors.

6. A commitment to work collaboratively not only with the known adults in the school but also with unknown artists from the community.

7. Time must be set aside for children's ideas to be included

and for them to develop their work to a high level of quality

8 Teachers must have high expectations and be able to support children in responding to the challenge and excitement of work on carnival.

9 Carnival should not be seen as a one off event but as potentially a regular part of the school curriculum developed and refined over the years.

I will end with a quote from the teacher and calypsonian Hollis Liverpool.

"I have pointed out the need for the gaining of attitudes and values which are important if we are to produce educated citizens who will respond adequately in this multiracial society. It calls for teachers with a sense of purpose and dedication. It calls for teachers conscious of their roots who understand the problem of identity of Caribbean peoples; teachers who see the beauty of art; teachers who realise that culture is a magnificent force, the soul of the people. It is indeed a big task so above all it calls for teachers who do not depend solely on the Ministry of Education for guidance but who are alive to the demands of a broadened and changing curriculum and will rise to take the bull by the horns. So gentle reader I commend carnival to you for all that it is worth. Dear teacher, I give you the greatest show on earth". ▪

Clary Salandy Mahogany Arts

I never stop thinking about what could possibly be the next carnival theme. There's always something that's going to happen, and I don't have a problem with changing the theme a few months before Carnival if something that I think is more important happens.

Sometimes I will choose a theme to capture what is going on in the Mas camp. For example, one year I did a band that was called, 'All the Colours of the Rainbow' which came out of little things that had happened in the Mas Camp. We had mixed race people in our membership. There was the Nation of Islam shop down the road, and we had a bit of a discussion with one of them. We were saying that a person could not be aggressive towards white people, especially if their mother was white and their father black.

So 'All the Colours of the Rainbow' used colour to say, orange is just as beautiful as yellow and red, and orange is the mix of the two. So what the hell are we worried about here, in this race thing, basically?

That's one way of finding a theme, the other way of course is some major incident. When there was the massacre in Tiannemen Square, we did a wonderful costume called, 'Shadow over Tiannemen Square' and I just changed the whole theme of the band, because I wanted to do that costume, that year. You grab the moment to show what a voice carnival can be, and it also showed solidarity with the Chinese community.

'Some Come To Jump Up, Some Come To Party'

Sound, Emotion and Discovery at Notting Hill Carnival

Geraldine Connor
MMus, LRSM, Dip Ed

Thousands of people...

Geraldine Connor
is an ethnomusicologist and Senior Lecturer at the University of Leeds, specialising in all aspects of popular music performance. She also writes and advises on many aspects of carnival practice as well as working as a player and arranger within the steelband movement. Geraldine composed and directed 'Carnival Messiah', a radical theatrical reinvention inspired by George Friedrich Handel's oratorio 'Messiah'. Whilst on secondment, Geraldine has also held the post of Associate Director (Music) to the West Yorkshire Playhouse.

...all moving with a collective rhythm...a blend of sounds and smells...rum, rice 'n' peas, beer, excited chatter, ackee and saltfish, cologne, Kentucky Fried Chicken, fry plantain, laughter, sweat! The insistent, consistent, percussive rhythm of steel band in the distance... ragga, soca and hip hop throbbing...from huge speakers and passing 40 foot articulated lorries...at a decibel level that insists on engraving the lyrics on your brain...as you, scream along with the lead singer... you are engulfed in a sea of sound and motion...wave after wave of bass, riddum' and heights bombard your body, mind and soul...you are alone...but you are not alone...everything is excluded but the sound...shoulder to shoulder...back to back...belly to belly...your body...their bodies...respond in primal instinct...to a gamut of sonic emotion...as you journey freely through the corridors of Notting Hill Carnival...enwrapped on a voyage of sound and discovery....

The carnival tip begins months before the actual event. Masquerade band launchings, carnival clubs and fetes feature all the top London DJ's and current soca music hits, most originating in Trinidad and Barbados and then to a lesser extent (with the exception of Byron Lee) the rest of the Caribbean.

On the road, mobile sound systems play predominantly recorded soca music on CD, MP3, DAT, mini disc and Vinyl format. With very few exceptions, this music is performed by well known calypsonians and bands from the West Indies. As Notting Hill Carnival takes place approximately six months after the Trinidad Carnival and one month after the Barbados Crop Over, it is possible for all the current calypso and soca trends to be adopted and adapted for use by the Notting Hill Carnival masquerade bands.

The mobile sound systems, of no less than 20 kilowatts of manually generated power, are usually set up on 40 foot open-sided articulated trucks or trailers and slowly driven or hauled by tractor through the streets of Notting Hill. In terms of equipment and operation they are essentially made up of the same components as the static sound systems.

Static sound systems have been officially associated with the Notting Hill Carnival since 1975, but have been part of the carnival milieu since its inception in the late 1950's. Today, sound systems are hi-tec and hi-powered systems of sound generation that are often custom-built to accommodate very specific sound separation requirements. The modern sound system can set up in any available large space near a power line. There are usually at least four speaker systems set up around the perimeter. The 'control tower' consists of power amplifiers, crossovers, turntables, tape recorders, mixers, FX (effects) rack and microphones.

At Notting Hill Carnival, the current repertoire of the sound systems depends on which specialist music the sound system's leader prefers. Sound system personnel usually include one or more DJs/ Toasters/ Talk-over artistes/ MCs and a selector, who chooses the music. Quite often, a 'sound' will have several teams on hand who specialise in different music.

Notting Hill Carnival statistics reveal that over 60% of carnival spectators go to the carnival to listen to the sound systems. It has been mooted that the reasons why so many people come to the carnival is that it's free music all day, and there are lots of other activities if you are interested. The most recent trend however, has been for West End and other trendy Club DJs to play at the Carnival thus attracting their regular punters to the event.

The British Association of South Systems (BASS) was constituted to address the very real need for formalising the sound systems operations within the carnival arena, dealing with such matters as power supplies, health and safety issues and sound dimensions. Approximately fifty sites within the carnival area are provided for the sound systems and every effort is made to keep them away from the main masquerade band routes so there is no conflict of live versus recorded music, soca versus any other non appropriate masquerade music.

The static sound system came into existence in the late 1940's in Jamaica and consisted of portable sets of record decks, powerful amplifiers and huge banks of speakers that played in yards and dance halls to paying customers. Initially they played imported American rhythm and blues but then certain sound systems proprietors began to record their own exclusive discs.

This was the birth of the Jamaican recording industry of which the earliest products were intended purely for the use of the sound system. By the 1960's, the most important elements of the modern sound system had been developed. The custom of dancing to portable recorded music, the development of records especially tailored to the needs of the disco and additionally, a new role for DJs as the main focus of the music rather than a mere announcer.

These sound systems provided an opportunity for the grassroots people to talk back, to choose, to respond and each system had its own toasting/ DJ heroes who could express the feelings of the crowd. Often the DJ or talk over artiste, like the calypso singer helped to clarify local opinion on pressing social and political issues.

In fact, the Jamaican disco or sound system is in many ways the most vital element in the modern development of reggae music. Though for many years often down played and misunderstood outside of Jamaica, the dances serviced by these sound systems continue to be the most significant outlet for reggae music in both Jamaica and Britain. It can be said that reggae music (rooted in the long retained traditions of African Burru drumming and Rastafarian theology) is really a fusion of these retained traditions with a number of other musics. Even more notably, it has successfully coupled with those deeply tribal technological instruments, the transistor radio set, the recording studio and the gigantic sound system.

The history of Jamaican music in Britain is the history of various Jamaican born styles (notably ska, rock steady and rockers) transported to an alien culture and once there, gradually shedding their Caribbean mores and developing a distinct and individual identity. Between the decades of the 1950's to 1970's, Jamaicans in Britain made a deliberate effort to only listen to, copy and master Jamaican musical initiatives. However by the early 1980's, during a period of growing self-affirmation and self-confidence amongst the black youth of Britain, a conscious desire that had been developing quietly in the background of other social changes came to fruition. This was the establishment of a purely British black reggae music style; it was called 'fast style'.

In the 1940's, the nearest thing to a Jamaican popular music style was 'mento', a calypso-like, Latin influenced folk music with a gentle, lilting melody and topical, sometimes mildly bawdy lyrics. Two other musics flourished at that time: the religious expression of Rastafari accompanied by Burru drumming; and the music that was broadcast via short-wave radio from the Florida belt of the Americas. In the late 1950's, Jamaica's unique interpretation of this popular American rhythm and blues sound resulted in the birth of 'ska'.

Ska, the street music of poor Kingston, was played on electric guitars, drum kit and usually a small brass section. Its distinctive musical feature was the stabbing, syncopation of the piano and guitar chords accented on the second and fourth beats of the bar. Most important however, was the fact that with the new rhythm came a new message and the message was about poverty, inequality, black identity and cultural resistance.

In 1965, a new Jamaican popular music style came into being. Dub, as it was called, was simply a rhythm track without solo. By the late 1960's, along with the development of the DJ as an artiste in his own right, and by emphasising the bass and drums as well as introducing sound effects, dub developed a separate and very popular style.

In 1966, rock steady changed the format of ska to include a more specifically Jamaican experience whilst simultaneously absorbing vocal and instrumental influences of black America. However, by late 1967, the rhythm was changing from a slow meditative beat to a walking pace, with the bass even more prominent. This style became known as reggae. Reggae achieved international recognition and remained popular throughout the 1970's and early 1980's.

This era saw the rise of two vocally grounded styles, the first new style was espoused by the Dub Poets. Their trademark was to recite their verse using reggae backing or reggae influenced vocal rhythms. The second was the ascendance of the DJ/toaster, who developed the art of rendering a stream of improvised lyrics over a specially recorded backing track that was often the 'dub' version B-side of a record. In some cases they would

'call' over the record itself, competing and interacting with the lead vocalist.

After the death of Bob Marley in 1981, Roots reggae fundamentalists refused to tolerate any new music input. They would only allow experimentation within the narrow confines provided by 'heavy' or 'African' rhythms. The music had been stripped down to its purest form. Jamaica must have felt that they were loosing 'their' music. They had already lost their idol Marley, so logically, their music would be next to go. In an effort to preserve the music they turned inward towards the 'tradition' that had served them so well in the past.

Reggae would only be renewed and refreshed if it was combined again with other forms of music. In Britain this was a lesson they were learning fast, the next style to emerge in the early 1980's was lover's rock, a soft, non-political, lyrical ballad music.

Then, in 1984, Dub Vendor released a DJ reggae record featuring Smiley Culture singing 'Cockney translation'. This was a landmark in British reggae. It was called "fast-style" and was seen as reggae's answer to rap. The toaster/DJ would either deliver his lines to a light tight beat pushed out by a drum machine, quite the opposite to dub or lover's rock, where reggae got slower, fast style got faster.

In Jamaica however, a most crude style had evolved. It was called 'dancehall' and led by DJs who espoused 'slackness'. The chat became increasingly concerned with crude sex talk, displaying a remarkably deep-seated fear and distrust of women. By the second half of the 1980's, record producers began using samples and backing tracks from existing records. This developed into a style called 'digital dancehall', in which a voice, a computerised keyboard and a drum machine were the only ingredients. The Jamaican reggae music industry had recovered. The 1990's saw dancehall renamed as "ragamuffin'" or "ragga" as it is more commonly known, in acknowledgement of its young audiences of latter-day rude buoys. The ragga style is chanted over soul backing tracks and reggae singers and DJ's are teaming up to perform duets. Most recently the DJs have combined with American hip hop.

Whereas reggae is bound up with the idea of roots and culture, rap is rooted in the experience of lower class blacks in the U.S.A's big northern cities. The culture that grew up around rap, 'hip hop', involves dance, image/style, language and wild style graffiti, but, at its core, it involves attitude. Rap did for poor blacks in America, what reggae did, a decade earlier, for disenfranchised West Indians in Britain.

In 1967, a DJ called Herc Kool emigrated to the U.S.A. from Jamaica, moving into the West Bronx. Here he got to know the Jamaican sound system scene, and bought his own sound system. As he was already familiar with the early talk over artistes, he was able to quickly make a name for himself as an up and coming DJ. He found however that the New York black crowd would not respond to reggae so he began talking over the Latin funk styles that he knew would appeal to them.

Gradually he developed a style that was so popular that he began buying records only for the instrumental breaks rather than for whole tracks. Rather than play the whole record straight through he would play the same part several times over, cutting from one record deck to the other as he 'chatted' through the microphone. This had two consequences. Firstly, he had to buy several copies of each record he used and secondly, he had to develop a phenomenal sense of timing. He used the headphones that DJ's use to cue their music so that he could cut from one copy of a record to another at exactly the right point.

The style Herc Kool invented became known as 'break beats'. Switching between record decks got faster and more complicated and as Kool was unable to rap and operate the records at the same time, he employed two MCs who would dance in front of the decks, bouncing lines off each other. They became the first MC dance team.

The inclusion of a hip hop oriented repertoire with the sound systems in the Notting Hill Carnival celebrations is not as unrelated to Caribbean carnival culture as it first appears. ■

Bro Linton & Ras Benji

Sunday 29 August 1999 about 5.30am. I was busy readying myself getting prepared for the day ahead. I was organising my bags of African crafts while waiting for my cousin to collect me, making sure that I'd not forgotten something. My cornmeal porridge was bubbling away on the cooker; the bath was nearly set. By the time I'd finished, my cousin Linton phoned to say that there would be a bit of a delay before his arrival. When he turned up Wayne was there ever ready as usual. Wayne was driving the van; I went along in my cousin's car. Raymond was down from Doncaster with his wife Bev the sister of Sheila my cousin's wife. My cousin and I went to collect Jenny and Ryan and would meet up with the rest on route at Camberwell Green.

By the time we arrived they had still not obtained all the food items. We needed some flour, plantains, cooking oil and a few other food stuffs. Eventually we got under way heading towards Oval, Victoria, Hyde Park, Notting Hill and on to Ladbroke Grove. We took our usual turn off point at Chepstow Road and went through the police cordons.

While passing through the streets making our way to the pitches, I noticed some familiar faces. People were hurriedly setting up their pitches, eagerly waiting for the crowds to arrive. Having unpacked rather hastily my cousin went to park up the van while we got on with setting up the stalls.

This year we ran two adjoining stalls as opposed to the usual one. We had decided to sell food as well as African arts and crafts in order to offer choice and variety. Wayne was busy setting up the jerk drum in readiness of the fish and chicken. Ryan and Raymond were sorting the different sections of the stall. I was sorting out the individual boxes which each contained various works of art. By now my cousin had returned and was helping to sort out the other necessities. I had just started to put out some books when, the first of the browsers arrived. They were two foreign women they were extremely excited about the African carvings, they spent quite a while looking at the earrings before buying a few pairs.

The first sounds of music could now be heard on the street. Mickey from Channel One sound system was soundchecking. The street was getting busier I could now smell the sweet aroma of food drifting in the air. Fried dumplings, saltfish fritters, grilled sweet corn. It was all happening and all the hurdles faced in getting here were forgotten.

Designing for Carnival

Interview

 Carlton Garcia    Pax Nindi

Trinidadian born **Cali** is a costume design specialist and has over 15 years experience of working with Peter Minshall. He has worked in the UK for the past 6 years with Kinetika Arts and mas bands such as Yaa Asantewaa, Mahogany, Beeraahar Sweet Combination and South Connections. His work outside of Notting Hill Carnival has included assisting Mahogany Arts in the production of the centre piece for the Millennium Dome and Kinetika Arts at Ryde Carnival, Isle of Wight.

PN If you start by telling me what you're doing in England, which people you've worked with etc.

CG My friends call me Cali. I've been coming to England for the past 5 or 6 years, coming to do Notting Hill Carnival, working with a couple of groups in England. I work with Yaa Asantewaa and I have worked with Mahogany doing the centre-piece of the Millennium Dome. I then went to Singapore with Mahogany to the Chinge festival. I also briefly worked with South Connections as well as Beeraahar Sweet Combination Club.

PN And in Trinidad, which clubs did you work with?

CG I've been working with Peter Minshall for 14 or 15 years. A friend of mine used to work with Callaloo and he knew I liked to sew fabric. That's my main thing. So I started working with this friend and I loved making the costumes. Minshall had a different technique that is always above the rest. Aside from working with the band, you always learn something from Peter Minshall.

I also did some work, in the early days with a smaller steel band in Trinidad. We did sailor mas and war mas. I did a couple of costumes for customers and again liked it, got into it and started co-designing sections for the steel band. After that I moved onto Callaloo and ever since I've stayed with Minshall.

PN Is there anyone in England that you would compare to Minshall?

CG No, sorry to say, but no. There are good designers at Notting Hill Carnival, but no! Minshall also studied in England, I should probably say that, so there is a link.

PN Why is there nobody like him in England, do you think?

CG I have great respect for Minshall as far as design and techniques go. I haven't seen anyone match up to his techniques and his designs here. In fact a lot of bands use Minshall's techniques. A lot of wings in NHC are made of silk and that kind of thing. Minshall was the first person to do stuff with wings. He was the first person to design costumes that you wear, rather than costumes that move on wheels. He's a trend-setter. You can see Minshall's work all over London when you look at Notting Hill Carnival.

PN Having worked with carnival clubs in England, how do they compare with each other? For example, do you think there are serious differences between Yaa Asantewaa, Mahogany and South Connections?

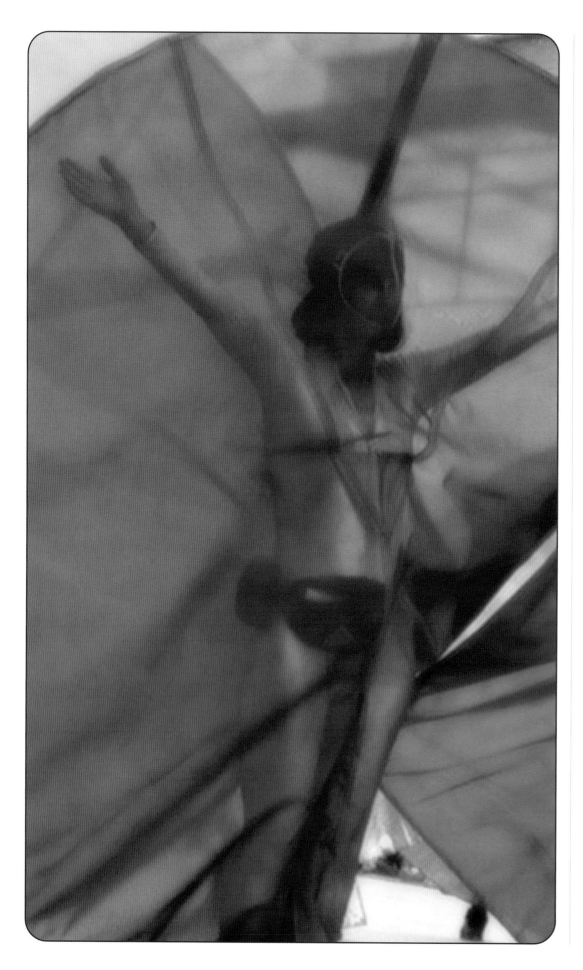

CG Well, Mahogany's style is close to the Minshall style. Recently they've started using a lot of fabrics, and fabric is along Minshall's vein, like silks and beads. Yaa Asantewaa brings people over from Trinidad. I work with Yaa and I'm from Trinidad. We all work with Minshall's camp, so that's the first connection as far as Minshall's influence on Notting Hill Carnival goes. South Connections hire a couple of people from Minshall's camp to do some costumes, so that's where that influence is coming from. Clary at Mahogany is from Trinidad and Speedy is a Minshall person. A lot of the techniques used by Mahogany's instructors are based on what Speedy learnt in Trinidad. There are also other influences in England. For example, Cocoyea's costumes are different as they are more of a bikini style.

With Minshall, when you wear a costume, it says something. You can look at a costume know that it represents something. It's part of something that can tell a story and that's the difference to me between Minshall and the rest of the bands.

PN If somebody came to you today and said they want to know about making costumes, what would be your advice to them? What would they need from scratch?

CG OK, first what they will need to have is a concept. People take concepts from different things. It could be a personal idea that you have or a vision that you want to bring into reality. It could be something that's happening, like politics or just a butterfly. You like how it looks and you decide, hey I could use that idea! Then you've got your context. Research is very important at this stage. This can be done through the internet or the library. Then as an artist you can put the images that come into your head on paper and that's the next step. When it's on paper you look at it, you can make changes until you're happy with it. Then you make a prototype to make sure that the design is workable. With small costumes it's easier. As for large costumes, you need to have some experience with structure. If you design a large costume you need to know how it's going to stand up, how it's going to fit on the person, how it's going to balance properly, so you have to design with that knowledge. You shouldn't do a design that wouldn't work as a costume. Then you choose fabrics and you find materials. I like to use things that are available. I like to see things recycled, things you can re-use.

PN Having worked in Trinidad and England, are there problems find-ing materials? Is either country better in terms of finding materials?

CG I would say Trinidad has nice fabrics; we bring materials from Trinidad to England. There are fabrics in England but their availability is poor. You don't have a carnival store that has all sorts of stuff we use for carnival, such as trimmings, glitter etc

PN You've got your concept and your theme, sketches and you've got everything you need, in terms of making say for example, the butterfly, how would you start to make it?

CG First you do a pattern. Scale your drawing depending on how big or small you want it; maybe on plastic with proper measurement and points where your rods are going. Then you cut your silk on the plastic, so you can see through (which is one reason why you use plastic). Mark where your rods are going, cutting tunnels for your rods. Then you make your fibreglass backpack. You can also use metal or aluminium, it depends on what kind of strain the backpack has to take. You make a mould out of Plaster-of-Paris on the person who's wearing the costume. Then you coat the mould with fibreglass on the inside to make a frame. We then cut an aluminium shape that fits in a slot on the backpack itself. Say your wings are separate, you have your backpack on and you take your wings and slot into the backpack and they hang from there. Once you've worked all this out, you sew your wings up. You might want to paint it, or dye them, depending on the type of butterfly you are making. There are other costumes that will take other techniques according to the design you have. You might have to develop techniques to make that design work.

PN Does it matter what space you're using?

CG Yes, it does matter. You need enough space, at least when you're making a large costume. It all depends on what the costume is. You make it in a way that can be stored so that when it's finished it can be stored properly. If the costume is 15ft high and 14ft wide you will need a space three or four times bigger than that to be able to make the costume.

PN When you have worked in Trinidad and worked in England, do you find here that people have problems finding space, or there's not much difference?

CG The people I've worked for so far have been alright with space. Yaa Asantewaa use their centre. Mahogany has their place and shop-front. South Connections has their own space. I haven't seen a problem with the people I've worked with. I did visit other Mas camps and I know there are other people with space problems. I see some fellows making costumes in really small spaces and I know that's really uncomfortable. You can't do your best if you don't have a space.

PN How important is the Mas camp? When you are talking about a Mas camp, do you look at it like a workshop or a place where people meet and do other things?

CG Well, two things. People tend to look at carnival and costume making as just a fun thing. When most people look at carnival costumes, they are not aware of the amount of organising involved especially in the mas camp. There's also a good atmosphere in the mas camp because people meet sometimes once a year, so you come to work and have fun. There are some people who just come to make costumes, learn something and help, come after work and feel a part of the band. When they get on the road, they feel like, yeah, that's my band. It's a nice atmosphere. It is a business but the atmosphere can't be in a straight jacket situation. You wouldn't flow, it's a vibe, making carnival costumes, the Mas camp vibe, you need to have that vibe in order to really get the best out of the whole thing and do your best.

PN Is the atmosphere in Mas camps in Trinidad and England roughly the same in the places you've worked in? If they're different, what's different?

CG Yaa Asantewaa is the closest to the Trinidad Mas camp. I've worked with Ali Pretty from Kinetika. For example, I did the Luton carnival and the Thames festival with her. They have that kind of vibe. You know, more of 'Trini' kind of vibe. There's no "you're a designer, you're this", we are all a nice team. I think that's the closest to the Minshall camp, we have that kind of closeness.

PN How accessible is a Mas camp? Could anyone walk in off the street into Minshall's Mas camp or South Connections Mas camp?

CG Yes, Minshall's Mas camp is always open, as far as I know and so is South Connections. You're welcome as long as you don't get in the way. You come, learn things and help, some people come in and volunteer, just to learn and be part of a band.

PN At the moment there's a thing about sizes, that England is making larger costumes than Trinidad?

CG I think England is coming up to par with Trinidad as far as large costumes are concerned. I've seen some really good costumes in England, big ones, not just our costumes, but other bands have

created some really great and large costumes. The only problem with Notting Hill Carnival is the space and crowds. My opinion is that carnival, in Notting Hill, is about costumes, doing a band, spending all those nights and money on making costumes, it's about showing the costumes and a street parade. What I've found coming here over the years is that the crowds keep narrowing the route, the costumes can barely get through, they have to go sideways. One other thing about Notting Hill Carnival that is upsetting to me is the judging point. The costumes can't even fit on the judging point, it's really tiny. I think if we spend a lot of money making costumes when you get to the grand finale there should be no obstacles. It's a personal thing that I have that really bothers me.

PN And in Trinidad?

CG In Trinidad, the Savanna is the main stage and it's about roughly 400 yards of stage and is really wide and there's another judging point down town. In Trinidad, carnival is a national thing, not an area kind of thing, so anywhere in Trinidad you can do a band and have a street parade. So it starts all over, you have a route, all the way down town to one judging point, up town to another then head up to the grand Savanna where the main competition is. Before you get to the Savanna, the actual stage, there's at least a mile, that's inside the Savanna, for you to get organised and in line to cross the stage. Space, that's what Trinidad has compare to England. When you say street parade, it is a street parade.

You can parade from your area, round town up to the Savanna, then back to your Mas camp. You start from 8am and reach the end of the route by about 5pm. There are all these hours of parade and not this jammed-up situation. Of course when it's close to the Savanna you get bands lining up but it's not jammed.

PN Let's compare the elements between England and Trinidad. In England we have soca on the move, the Calypsonians, steel pan, masquerade and sound systems. How does this compare with Trinidad or Brazil where they don't have sound systems like Notting Hill Carnival.

CG My opinion is that Notting Hill Carnival isn't Trinidad Carnival. We are West Indian people, we have African people, different people from different parts of the world, your taste is different, you like different music. I think it's about music. We need more emphasis on the costumes, mas bands should be first priority. Then you have the sound systems a little bit away from the costumes. So people who like the sound systems can go to that area and enjoy that, and the people into the carnival and costumes will have a better, more comfortable area to parade and enjoy the carnival. It's fine, because it's your culture. I like music too but I like carnival, carnival mas is my first love, my being. If you totally separate them then you will get an ease-up on the congestion on the carnival route.

I think we need to keep the carnival costumes. A sound system must be

a registered costume band, not a registered sound system. It causes a lot of problems. You leave camp at 9, 10am and you know it's dark before you cross the judging point. A lot of times you have children in the band and it's unsafe to have kids staying until they cross the judging point. Getting them out of the band before it gets dark, they don't enjoy themselves.. I think it would help by regulating the sound systems and trucks, it's one of the best things they could do to ease up the congestion, if they have to stay on Ladbroke Grove. I think we need more space. Most mas men keep saying in London, we need more space, desperately need more space. It becomes more dangerous with all these people, and this narrow space to go through as people begin to push, so you don't enjoy the carnival really. I do love Notting Hill Carnival because of the different people, different races and styles of costume.

PN Most times in England when you say carnival they think NHC. I visit carnivals all over the UK and there are a lot of carnivals in this country. Some of them are based around the Trinidad style, others are based around the Asian communities, Chinese communities, many follow age-old English traditions. Do they have anything like that in Trinidad?

CG Oh yeah, there's a mixed culture in Trinidad

PN Is that reflected in the costume making? When you see a Trinidad carnival, do the costumes say Trinidad? Can you say there's a typical Trinidadian costume?

CG No, I wouldn't say that. There is a very big difference. I can look at a costume and know it's a West Indian style of costume. I don't want to say Trinidad all the time, as there's other Caribbean countries that do carnival. A lot of the influences come from Trinidad because that is the maker of carnival in the West Indies.

PN What happens to the costumes, to the maker, to the Mas camp after carnival is finished?

CG In Trinidad after carnival, people keep the smaller costumes if they've paid for them. Some people keep their costumes in their house, depending on whether they're carnival fanatics. The large costumes are kept in camp and we always have jobs to take the costumes all over the world. We do functions all over – Atlanta, John Michelle Jarre, and we always use the costumes over and over again. People call and ask for Tan Tan and Sailor Boy. Those two costumes are known world-wide, and they were done for carnival in Trinidad by Minshall for the King & Queen for the band Tan Tanner sometime in 1989 or 1990. To this day, those costumes still go all over the world, they've made more Tan Tan and sailor boy costumes for children. In fact, they made a whole Tan Tan and sailor boy family with puppets. You don't make your costume then throw away the next day. It does depend how good your costume is. Some people recycle, keep it for a year, and then you come in next year and use parts from the costume to create a costume for the next year.

PN So, in Trinidad you use the costumes again and if there's an exhibition you take it around the world. If there are sections then would you keep them all in one place or would they go to different individuals?

CG The section costumes bought by the wearers, so the costume is yours, you don't bring it back to the camp. If we need to do a show and we need section costumes, then we make new ones and they then belong to the Mas camp or the company that hires the costumes.

PN Do they do the same sort of thing in England?

CG Yeah, the bands I worked for keep some of their costumes. Yaa Asantewaa has problems with storage space. Almost all of the bands have problems with storage, so they make a costume and store it for two years. You can't store it properly, so it would get damaged. You'd have a job having to fix the costume again as it's not stored properly. So storage is a problem. I think the weather has a lot to do with it. Two things happen in Trinidad, sun and rain and they have seasons for it. So you can build a shed outside and have your costumes in it. You can't do that in England because of the weather and the law that you can't build a shed out the back of your house without planning permission. I feel really good when I make a costume. Me personally, when I work on a large costume especially, and I work really hard and sometimes get frustrated and fight it and you make it and you see the end result, I get a rush – it's almost as good as sex, honestly, that's my biggest satisfaction in making costumes.

PN In England, there are those major carnival clubs, like Mahogany, that make costumes all year round. Then there are those that just do it towards Carnival and then stop. They haven't got any money to carry on all year round so they either have to approach the Arts Council of England or the local authorities for funding. There are not many mas people who survive from just making costumes. In Trinidad what's it like, how does it compare with here?

CG It's different in Trinidad as far as finance towards costumes and carnival bands is concerned The government give a grant; they give prize money, a certain amount of money for second and third prizes, different categories and so on. You don't get grants to make costumes.

PN So you have to make it first, then you get a prize?

CG Yes, you make it, you enter the competition, you use your own money, it's a business. Before, a person would design and make their costumes with a seamstress, but since its got more high-tech and more modern, it's a different kind of thing really. You're a company, you have a capital, you invest, have a bank loan to create revenue and you buy your own materials. People come in, choose which section they want to play in and they pay for it. In Trinidad you have to pay the price of a costume. For example, a section costume would cost $400 to make and that costume would sell for a minimum of $500 and go up to $1800/$2000 for a large costume. The large costumes are more or less company costumes. Some people sponsor their own large costumes – it depends how much love you have for the mas. In England it's not that kind of vibe. I wouldn't say it's more of a community, but a grand kind of system. What I've seen in London is that if you make a costume and put a price on it, (adding up what you spend on making it, the cost and labour) you can't sell a costume for that price. I mean if you gave someone a price of a costume, they wouldn't pay for it, because it's not the kind of love. They're not as passionate about carnival.

You say 'do you wanna come with us and play in the band' and the next question is 'how much are you paying?', so it's a different kind of thing. Once people get to know what the real carnival vibe is, it will be better.

I've seen schools doing workshops; I'm seeing children interested in making costumes. I've done some workshops and it's really something for me. I hold this carnival knowledge, this costume thing and I like sharing that knowledge, showing someone something and they make it and seeing they are happy about it. I think that's one way that London is going right at the moment, getting the kids to actually make their own costumes. All we really have to do is guide them and they are really interested in making them. I did workshops in Luton for Luton Carnival, and the parents were encouraging, the kids were doing their stuff and I think England is going the right angle in terms of education. People don't really know about carnival, they feel the vibe but they don't know what it is really – like it's art and if you like art in any kind of way and you're making something out of nothing, there's an interest and people want to learn more and more. I've seen kids really happy and they wear their costumes and they're really proud and you hear them telling people 'I made my costume and Cali helped me to make it' and that's the kind of thing I really like. ▪

ON ROUTE

European Carnival Traditions and Evolutionary Change

Alan
Dix

For some, Europe is seen as the originator of carnival world-wide.

Alan Dix has worked in the arts for nearly 25 years. In the 1990s he produced the Bradford Carnival for the Bradford Festival. Alan has also established a number of touring performance networks including Black Country Touring, artSites Birmingham and On Tour in Greenwich. He managed over 200 millennium events for Greenwich Council and his company, 509 Arts, works with a range of national clients on cultural policy, strategy and management.

European carnival traditions are said to be older than any others, its links with pre-Christian and Roman culture easy to trace, and the European influences on Caribbean and South American carnival obvious to anyone who knows their history. There is much truth in this, but it's not the whole story. What is clear is that European carnival tradition may be different in feel and format from the carnival celebrations that take place in the Americas, but they are close blood relations. The huge popularity of Notting Hill Carnival and the influence it is beginning to have on other European carnivals is proof, if it is needed, that no tradition is pure, and that carnivals have always expropriated ideas from whenever and wherever they can. In the true spirit of carnival, traditions can be subverted for present need, and evolutionary change is almost part of the definition of what 'carnival' is.

This may not be apparent to carnivalists in Europe today. The mainland European carnivals which are known around the world today - Nice, Venice, Cologne, Viareggio being amongst the most famous - are enormous international affairs and major tourist attractions. With budgets of millions of euros and thousands of jobs dependent upon them, they are locked into the local economies of their host towns and cities.

Underpinning this industry is a sense of tradition that goes back centuries. European carnival families can trace their lineage through many generations and observe with pride the passage of carnival craft and art from father to son in what has been historically a very male world. It is ironic that a form representing political and religious satire, social anarchy and the inversion of role and status has an organised, competitive and hierarchical underpinning dependent upon the observance of social norms and traditions. In short, European carnivalists are often a conventional bunch, defending a celebration that has its roots in prehistoric social ceremony.

The human psyche has a fundamental need to explore its 'wild child'. The Romans during the feast of Saturnalia elected a King of Chaos, the festival of Fools was common throughout the middle ages and contemporary European carnival is packed with images of young devils. Not the Devil you understand, but demonic representatives of the domestic diabolic forces that torment us on a daily basis. Much of what carnival is about is the need to infringe, to be excessive, to unloosen, to indulge. Carnival occupies a twilight zone between the permitted and the prohibited. A safety valve where the under-class can release their feelings while the over-class allow themselves to be ritually humiliated and everyone gets to forget the cares of everyday life for a while. It

is tricky territory though, and the danger of the whole situation getting out of control is obvious. That is why carnival has dodged in and out of acceptability. Carnival is revolution for a day, when the people take over the streets, when the normal codes of social behaviour are put away and the outrageous permitted. But let it not last any longer than its allotted time or trouble will ensue. The carnival at Romans-sur-Isère, southern France, in 1580 ended in a bloodbath after the ritualised rivalry got out of control. The Roman Catholic Church tried to ban the Feast of Fools and failed, and in the late 19th Century the authorities in Georgia (Russia) banned the carnival for its overt anti-Tsar sentiments. Authority is tested by carnival: it likes the idea of ring-fenced revolution, but doesn't know how strong the fence posts are. Consider the years of ambivalence that Notting Hill Carnival had to endure before it gained acceptance, despite the fact that its the biggest British carnival ever known.

Up to the 19th century there were very strong animist tendencies in carnival. At the core of many carnivals were hunts and fights, people dressed in animal skins, garlands and wild masks. It was pagan and it was carnal cleansing. Christianity provided the focus: a few days of excess before the repentance of Lent, a reminder that we are all sinners before the castigation of the priests.

On the whole, European carnival is now quite tame compared with some of the more excessive events in its past. It was tamed by spectacle, and it was the Italians who did it.

In the eighteenth century, the Italians began to combine the wild street theatre of carnival with pageantry and the influences of commedia delle arte. Whilst the profane elements of satire were retained, a more cultured and formalised structure began to emerge, with vast floats acting as the sets upon which known characters, such as Pierrot, strutted and improvised their way through the streets. This flux of influences, some very ancient, others more modern have an appeal that seems to be resilient and able to ride the tide of social change. The elements of ritual and historical legacy provide fixed points around which innovation is allowed to co-exist. Satire has its place, and the spectacular floats can

offer ridicule within a safe context of artistry. Masks, costume and make-up offer anonymity for those citizens who wish to abandon social convention for a short time whilst assuring them that they will be able to re-occupy their places in society once the partying is done.

None of this of course undermines the magic, nor the individuality, of each of the major European carnivals. From Viareggio, with its vast animated floats, each carefully crafted and populated by hundreds of costumed citizens, to the armies of grosse tetes that fill the streets of Nice, every European carnival has a distinct flavour which separates it from that of its neighbours.

What is changing however, is the place that the major carnivals now occupy in the tourism calendar throughout Europe. Carnival is no longer a simple celebration of the audacious, by local people. With the exception of the UK, it is a multi-million euro industry, supported by local and state taxes, driven by economic need and marketed in a connected global media environment. There is a danger that carnival will be forced by these processes to become ever more sanitised and consumable, held hostage by its own heritage and rendered impotent, unable to change. Market forces are now the greatest threat that European carnival has to face. Whether it will be able to continue to provide a philosophic, irreverent, anti-establishment view of the world whilst managing to enter the mainstream of big business Disney-style culture is anybody's guess. Let's hope that the needs of ordinary people, those who are still prepared to spontaneously populate the streets in a celebration of the untameable and the chaotic, will confound those who wish to turn European carnival into good tele-visuals, fast sound bites and even faster bucks. Only time and the streets of Europe will tell. ▪

H Patten

I had trained in traditional African dances with the National Dance Troupe in Ghana. After training I came back to England where I worked with international artistes from Africa and the Caribbean. As my career was just taking off, I got the opportunity to choreograph a production called, 'The Black Jacobeans', giving me a chance to work with Yvonne Brewster. This seemed like a big opportunity! In those days, as an artiste, the idea of being able to get your equity card was very important. But then I also had the opportunity to go to Trinidad for Carnival, and I had to weigh it up. Do I put my career forward by doing 'Black Jacobeans'? Or, do I put it forward by doing a research on carnival?

In the end, it was a laboured decision, but it still was quite an easy one because the attraction of going to Carnival won out. When we got to Trinidad, passing around the Savannah, the feeling and the air, you just knew something was happening. Carnival wasn't just about the two days, it was the whole build up.

For the first time, I experienced steel orchestras playing in Panorama, how they would make your heart strings vibrate in the same way that a sound box would when you go to a Blues dance. And then when you'd go to the Calypso tents you see the Calypsonians all preparing their songs and having their competition to see who's going to be the best. I remember looking at how the visual arts came to life when I went to the King and Queen competition, where you could see these sculptures in motion. It was so creative to see how people could develop a theme and push it to its very limit.

That was the power Carnival had and it gripped me straight away.

The steel pan instrument was born out of a poor nation, oppressed by the European plantation owners who ruled Trinidad and Tobago at that time.

Pepe Francis is currently manager and chairman of Ebony Steelband. He is also Honorary President of the London Brotherhood of Steel. During the 1980's, Pepe was administrator of the Notting Hill Carnival & Arts Committee. He continues to advise carnival organisers throughout the UK.

Like most of the oppressed of that era, rhythmic music and dance was a refreshing past time. Instruments were hand made from the tamboo bamboo (tamboo being derived from the French word 'Tambour' meaning 'drum'). They were also made with bamboo and the biscuit drum (made from the drums that were used to pack biscuits by the Bermudez and Sunrise Biscuit Company). The conventional steel pans of today used to be created from the discarded oil drums from the oil companies in the oil fields.

No one is sure who invented the first steel pan note and research is still being carried out by Pan Trinbago to try and establish the facts. There is however some general agreement that the instrument emerged in an organised form for the first time during the second half of the 1930's.

Some names that are associated with the creation of the steel pan as an instrument with notes, are Winston Spree Simon, Ziggily, Elliot-Manette and Boots Philmore Davidson. Over the years, all the relevant parts of a conventional orchestra have been associated with the different types of steel pan instruments such as the Tenor Pan or Soprano, the Cello Pan, the Guitar Pan, the Bass Pan and so on.

As technology (with regard to pan manufacture) improved and became more refined, cleaner and sharper notes were created from these forty-five gallon steel oil drums. Today, drums are specially made by "Van Leer" and other companies at great cost. Pan tuners now use a strobe-tuning machine instead of the old tuning fork method or as in the very early days, by ear.

The steel band in the early days was the main ingredient of carnival. Each steel band had a mas band attached to it, hence the phrase 'mas and pan is carnival'. As time went on, steel bands began playing different types of music other than calypso which included classical, jazz, R&B, pop etc. These tunes were picked up from the radio or from the Americans on the military base at Chaguaramas (West Trinidad).

The growth of steel bands in Trinidad and Tobago gave rise to bands like Red Army, Casablanca, Tokyo and Invaders to name but a few. In the past being a pan-man was considered a 'badman' thing due to the many conflicts between rival bands. However steel pan today is the national instrument of Trinidad and

Tobago, and most people want to be associated with it. 'Pan' to the pan-man ' is like a Jumbee (spirit), it gets in your blood'.

By the 1950's there were over eighty steel bands in Trinidad. In 1951 Edric Connor arranged for the Trinidad All Stars Percussion Orchestra (TASPO) to be the first steel band to travel to Britain to take part in the festival of Britain at the South Bank Complex. There were twelve pannists selected from over seventy steel bands across Trinidad. These were the pioneers of steel band music, selected to represent the island of Trinidad and Tobago in it's first ever steel band music venture in England.

The band was conducted by Lieutenant Joseph Griffith and its debut was on the 26th July 1951 in an open air performance. Tunes like Return of the Allies composed by Griffith, Tennessee Waltz, Cradle Song lullaby (Brahms), Sonny Boy (Jolson), Serenata serenade (Toscelli) were just a few of the many that started the birth of the steel pan in England.

Many of the TASPO members returned to Trinidad and then came back to England to continue playing steel pan music in England even if only in a small way, forming what we call 'gig sides'. A lot of the TASPO men were also pan tuners, in fact ten out of the twelve chosen were able to tune pans. So within a few years steel pan music started to grow in the United Kingdom. Many other pan-men started immigrating to England and though they were doing other jobs, steel pan music was always going to be their first love and their destiny.

In 1961, the College Boys Band "Dixieland" were creating history back in Trinidad, they were and still are the first and only band to win all four sections of the music festival. For this achievement they got the opportunity to come to England to perform over the Whitsun Bank Holiday weekend in 1961. They were the first steel band to travel throughout Europe and to Africa, organised from England by the great impresario of mas, pan and dance - Sonny Black.

The first steel band to participate in Carnival was Nostalgia Steel Orchestra. By 1969 there were more bands starting to emerge, Melody Makers, Blue Notes and Bay 57.

In 1969, Islington Green School started the first steel band in a school, under the guidance and teaching of Gerald Forsythe. That paved the way for a number of Inner London Education Authority (ILEA) Schools to start up steel pan classes and by 1975 there were over fifty schools. By then, Gerald Forsythe and Frank Rollock had formed the Pan Teachers Association, which was given recognition by the Greater London Council (GLC) in 1975. In 1978, Gerald Forsythe was appointed steel band organiser for schools, with an office at GLC headquarters, Waterloo near the South Bank. By 1990, Gerald had one hundred and sixty schools with steel pan as part of their curriculum. Some achievement considering that in Trinidad, the birthplace of steel pan, it was not yet considered to be a subject in schools.

While all this was happening, steel bands were growing in London,

Coventry, and Leeds (under Arthur Francis), Manchester, Liverpool and Huddersfield. The major bands were in London. By 1971 Metronomes and Ebony were competing in Carnival for supremacy both in music and costume on the road.

The first ever Panorama competition, held in 1978, was won by Paddington Youth. This band started in 1974 along with the London All Stars and was led by Frank Rollock. In 1976 Lambeth Youth led by Ricky Decarios appeared, now known as Southside Harmonics led by John Foster.

The Mangrove was always an institution in North Kensington. The Mangrove Association and the All Saint's Road go together like hand and glove and they attracted Trinidadians and people from all over the Caribbean islands. This was a home run by Frank Critchlow, so it was no surprise to see the Mangrove Steel Band rise up from a small, pan-round-neck steel band to be one of the biggest steel bands in England under the leadership of Clive (Mashup) Philip.

These were the bands that were carrying on the tradition of steel pan music in England. Similar to its birthplace Trinidad, steel bands developed a musical pride and so every year the players of the bands looked forward to London's Notting Hill Carnival and in particular the National Panorama competition. It's the one thing that kept and which still keeps steel bands together and it has caused new steel bands to be formed.

To give a brief outline of these bands and some of their achievements I have to return to the band Nostalgia, who were the first steel band to participate in Carnival in England. Then there is Ebony, who were the first conventional steel band to be formed in 1969.

In 1974 London All Stars Steel band was formed led by Frank (Jim Boots) Rollock. This band was and still is a family band, even though it is a teaching band and has members from all over London and even as far as Plymouth. Every member of the family plays steel pan, and they arrange their own music and can be relied upon to entertain an audience. Frank is a great Royalist and all his children have names with royal connections - the girls are Princess, Duchess, Countess and Elizabeth Rollock who has sadly passed away. The boys are King Rollock, Frank Junior and Philip Rollock. The family is a band in it's own right and everyone else who plays in London All Stars Steel Orchestra joins the family and that is unique.

In 1976 Lambeth Youth Steel Orchestra was formed led by Ricky Decarios. It was a small community band that was built up out of schools in South London. Ricky was a past-master at teaching children to play steel pan. I remember when they first appeared at the Tabernacle in Ladbroke Grove there were about twenty-five children between the ages of eight and thirteen, with a few older players no more than sixteen, and Ricky was always conducting with a tambourine in his hand. They have taken part in Panorama and have come close on a number of occasions, but so far the big one has eluded them. Today they are a big band called Southside Harmonics led by John Foster, under the musical direction of Eustace Benjamin formally of Metronomes.

In 1975 Bertram Parris left Metronomes and formed Glissando Steel Orchestra. In 1978 and under the musical direction of Pedro Burgess Glissando started participating in Panorama. But their main competition was the Steel Band Music Festival, which they won in 1981, 1982 and 1983. This competition was organised by 'The Greater London Council' (G.L.C.) in conjunction with the London Brotherhood of Steel which was formed to develop the interests of steel bands in London. Glissando dominated this competition for the first three years and after the demise of the GLC there were only two more competitions of this nature held. Glissando continued to pursue the coveted Panorama title, they had musical arrangers such as Dexter Joseph and Rudi (Two-Left) Smith in 1997 they came second.

In 1980 Mangrove Steel Orchestra was formed led by Clive Phillip and Boots Davidson. Raymond Joseph arranged all their festival music. They have won three Panorama competitions. In 1982, they tied with Metronomes. In 1986 they won Panorama under the musical direction of Rudi 'Two-Left' Smith. Today, the band is led by Matthew Phillip under the Musical Direction of Robert Clarke.

Metronomes Steel Orchestra was the band of the 1980's, formed around 1971 and led by Bertram Parris and Debeak, with the help of Emmerson the leader of the Metro youth club where they were based. Parris left the band in 1975 to form his own band but Metronomes continued under the musical leadership of Freddie Tossateau assisted by Eustace Benjamin, managed by Max Baden Semper.

There was also a steel band by the name of Groovers, led by Terry Noel who was always there in the background doing performances, but they never took part in Carnival or Panorama. In 1987 Phase One from Coventry came to London and under the leadership and musical direction of Victor Phillips they won the 1987 Panorama; it was one of the biggest upsets ever and it left the London bands feeling very dejected.

For a few years 1985 to 1990 Maestro's Steel Orchestra took part in Panorama. The band from Birmingham was led by Norman and Phillip Stewart. Maestro no longer functions as a band but Norman and Phillip still play and record steel pan music.

It is also worth mentioning that North Stars Steel Orchestra from Huddersfiled under the leadership of Kelvin Benjamin, started taking part in Panorama. The last two years (1991-92) Kenneth Guppy Brown was brought up from Trinidad to arrange their music. The band still exists today.

In 1982 Randolph Baptiste left Ebony to form Stardust Steel Orchestra and

in 1983 Stardust took part in Panorama for the first few years. They were a young band knocking on the door and in 1987 they came second to Phase One the band from Coventry.

Eclipse Steel Orchestra started in 1987, under the leadership of Dennis Osborne, with the help of Norton McClean and Haringey Youth Service. Philmore Boots Davidson was brought in to teach the band and they first took part in Panorama in 1990. Dennis then brought in Kirt Jagdeo, who took over the running of the band.

Pantonics Steel Orchestra was formed in 1988; their joint managers Ezekiel Biggs Yearwood and Raymond Joseph took them into Panorama in 1989. That was the year that Panorama was held at Wormwood Scrubs. Biggs tuned the pans and Raymond arranged the music. Sadly Raymond passed away but Biggs still carried on the band with the help of his son Grafton and Sam Springer (the then Mayor of Hackney). They now employ the services of Ian Beckles, a musical arranger from Trinidad who now lives in this country.

In 1969 a group of people from Trinidad decided they wanted to carry on playing steel pan music in England led by Randolph Baptiste, Cape James and Winston Pee Joseph. Ebony Steel Band was formed. They started rehearsals in an old garden shed at the back of Cape James House in Acton, much to the annoyance of his neighbours, who would sometimes throw stones on

top of the shed to try and disrupt the practice. As the band grew it moved to the Grenada Centre in Acton, there the band really took off.

When the band came out for Carnival in 1970, it was the largest steel band and costume band on the road. Ebony grew in leaps and bounds and won the Carnival King competition seven times and came second twice, a record yet to be broken. Ebony's followers came from far and wide. One of the largest sections came from Huddersfield and that section went on to start Huddersfield Carnival. Family members were also a great asset in the sewing of costumes and as the years went on the Quashie and Lewis family played a great part in

Ebony's overall success. Ebony moved to West London in 1977, to the Cryptic, a club in Paddington. By 1981 the Band had moved to Granville Centre in Queens Park Brent and in late 1981 to its present location in the centre of Carnival at Acklam Play Centre, located at the centre of Portobello Road under the A40 motorway.

All this time the big one, the National Panorama had eluded Ebony, they were the biggest band with supporters and mas players, and under the musical direction of Randolph Baptiste they tried year after year to win Panorama. In 1982, Pepe Francis decided to try a different arranger in consultation with

Randolph Baptiste, Earl Lewis and Cape James. A decision was made to employ Kenrick Isador as musical arranger for Panorama, which was the first year Ebony came in the first three. Randolph then left the band after the carnival of 1982 to form Stardust and Pepe Francis was left in charge as manager, with Earl Lewis as captain and Winston Joseph as chairman.

Pepe decided to bring aboard Geraldine Connor, a close friend and the classical music arranger to arrange the 1983 Panorama tunes. That was the first year Ebony won Panorama. That was the beginning of the Ebony success story. Ebony went on to become a charitable trust in 1988, responsible for the teaching of steel band music in schools also disabled workshops and music therapy in hospitals and mental institutions such as Dartford and Shenly. Ebony also has a young offenders institution programme. In addition, it trains tutors to be able to teach steel pan music in schools, and today degree courses in music can be obtained through playing steel pan in Ebony steel band at University College, Bretton Hall. This programme has been put in place by Geraldine Connor who is now a trustee of Ebony Steel band Trust and still organises a lot of our training projects.

Ebony then won Panorama in 1988 and 1989 and came second in 1990. This took place under the musical direction of Annise Halfer who came to Ebony after Geraldine Connor, and totally changed Ebony's style of music and playing. Hadeed was originally from Phase Two band in Trinidad but spent most of his time in England playing with the Breakfast Band and playing in Jazz festivals in the Caribbean, America and Europe with such musicians as Raff Richardson, Richard Bailey, Rudi Smith, Len Boogsie Sharp and Robbie Greenidge.

Ebony has won Panorama now for eight years in succession 1991-1998, a record that no other steel band has ever achieved. Renegades, the top steel band in Trinidad, has only ever won the Trinidad Panorama three times in a row.

Apart from the music and dedication of Ebony players, the other major reason for their success is the supreme quality of our instruments. This quality is attributed to Dudley Dickson who is thought to be the best steel pan tuner around today. Dudley takes pride in the pans he makes and is in great demand all over Europe.

David Grant Beeraahar Sweet Combination

I started playing steelpan in Guyana, with a band called Triple E in the early 1950s. One of the things that stands out for me in the time that I have been involved with Carnival was, when Ebony (Steel band) made the film Burning Illusion in 1978. When I started with Ebony there were only five members and by the time Burning Illusion was made Ebony was one hundred and seventy five member strong band.

Musically, I experienced a lot of excitement, through the musical sounds we made from a steel drum. At that time, a lot of competition existed among steel bands. Bands from Trinidad such as Desperado were at the top of the league, so entering the competition with bands of that status was really something. The fact that people wanted to make a film about Ebony showed that we were in that league.

Burning Illusion was filmed in a theatre in the West End and was never actually showed to us apart from being shown on the continent. However the experience itself, and what I learned during that time is what stands out in my mind.

In African societies, festivals play an important part in annual life. Festivals bring people together to celebrate something important in the life of the community.

Dr Frances Harding
is Lecturer in African Drama in the Department of African Languages and Cultures at the School of Oriental and African Studies, University of London. She has worked in theatre in various countries of Africa, particularly Nigeria, over many years and writes on several different aspects of theatre and performance in Africa.

Festivals bring people together During a festival everything that is ordinary becomes special. Thus in the first place, ordinary time is suspended, changed. For the duration of the festival, people do not engage in their ordinary business nor keep to their daily routines, but instead have days that stretch beyond the workday into night and beyond leisure time into a single whole that is a mixture of work and play. In order to mark out the period of the festival as special and different from everyday life, it has ritualised formalities at the beginning and end. These often take the form of sacred rituals — religious services asking for blessings on the forthcoming events.

Festivals are not random celebrations like a party, but like carnival, are built around a key event in the community's calendar. In some societies in Africa, it is the annual celebration of the New Yam, in others it is the annual remembrance of the ancestors, in yet others it is the annual thanksgiving for a good harvest and the preparatory rites for the next.

Sometimes festivals take place at the same time each year, as for example in the egungun festival of the Yoruba people of southwest Nigeria where the ancestors appear annually. Their appearance assures the living of their continued concern for them. The egungun are masked figures that process through the town, stopping to call at the homes of certain key persons on the route. The masked figures form part of a procession of performers of all sorts — acrobats, clowns, drummers, dancers, musicians.

Not all festivals take place annually however and some occur as and when they are needed for example a common reason for holding a festival is to hold celebratory ceremonies commemorating those who have died recently. These festivals are family events which take place after the deaths of elderly or other important relatives and because such festivals are expensive to stage, families usually wait for two or three years before announcing their intention to hold one. Such festivals as these may last for two or three days during the dry season, a time of the year when the demands of farming are less. There is dancing, music, masquerades, feasting and drinking.

Many of these features, religion, commemoration and celebration, are present in carnival. Whilst these are some of the ritual reasons why people in African societies hold festivals, the celebration generally goes well beyond the activities

directly required for the fulfilment of the ritual and becomes a major social occasion for the display of skill and talents in performance of all sorts. People seek to give honour by staging the best of everything in terms of performance and feasting. This brings in another aspect of festivals that is also present in carnival, their multi-layered nature. Festivals are not simple, single-stranded events, but draw together several meanings into a complex form of expression that is understandable on many levels — aesthetic, political, social and personal. Festivals are occasions when the disempowered are free to mock the powerful, when the private foibles and selfish antics of the well-known members of society are put on public display and held up to ridicule. Many last for several days and build up to a spectacular final event lasting throughout the night, turning night into day.

Just as ordinary behaviour and ordinary time is suspended for the duration of festivals, ordinary space is also transformed. The places where the festivals take place in African societies, may be ordinary spaces for most of the year, but during the festivals they become like a vast extended stage for a huge encompassing performance. Streets and village squares are turned into stages; shrines and palaces are decorated. It is in these spaces that all sorts of extraordinary things take place. Supernatural characters appear as masked figures to either reassure or frighten people. These masked figures are usually sacred characters and may be the dead returning as ancestors to assure the living of their continued concern. Alternatively, they may be spirits from the uncultivated land around the town or village who remind society of the dangers of the un-socialised wild surrounding them or else deities whose presence reminds people of a

life beyond that of the everyday. They are sacred characters because they are part of the religious beliefs of the particular society where they appear.

This preference for a processional form of performance and accompanying events is an essential part of the event, is present too in carnival. Performers move from a starting place to a finishing point. There is an emphatic use of the 'parade' as all the performers, the dancers, the masked characters, the musicians and other performers, start from one point and travel along an agreed route to end in another place. During the performance, the public space where they perform becomes the stage where the performers display their skills — a sign of the reversal of

things — a space where the powerless take over.

In Africa, masks have two possibilities: to reveal a character other than that of the wearer and to conceal the identity of the wearer. They are usually worn to temporarily bring supernatural beings into the human world. Masks are an important feature in the crossover between sacred and secular life. There are usually strict rules governing who is entitled to wear a mask. In most cases, it is young men who wear or 'carry' the masks, but they may only do so under certain conditions. There may need to be an appropriate family or kinship links or else be of a certain occupation. Alternatively, they may be required to

belong to a certain society whose rules and esoteric knowledge are kept from the rest of society. These are known as 'secret societies'. Lastly, they must be good performers, they must have skill at manoeuvring and dancing the heavy mask. By wearing certain masks, members of these societies bring into the community, those sacred presences that are not often visible in human society. They are sacred masks.

Masks are also one of the outstanding features of carnival and constitute a major area for the award of prizes. They are often very large structures encompassing not only the face but also the body and are surmounted by superstructures of lightweight materials. The extent of the structure frequently requires physical support beyond that provided by the wearer's head and shoulders. This takes the form of strong wire frames designed both as framework and support for the mask and costume. The resulting structures are fretworks of light, colourful materials elaborately decorated and embellished. Feathers, diaphanous textiles, reflective, silvery surfaces are preferred. In contrast to mask use in Africa, carnival masks surround the face of the wearer, but do not cover or conceal it, for the mask operates to highlight and draw attention to the wearer. In carnival, the performers seek ways of showing themselves in a special light, of displaying themselves and so the mask is used to elaborate and expand

on the wearer. There is no attempt to disguise and conceal the wearer, quite the reverse.

When so many performers come together and take over the normally ordered civic space, the opportunity to criticise public figures such as those in authority, or private citizens who have an exaggerated sense of their own importance is presented. Satirising civic dignitaries, Church authorities and hurling ribald humour at self-important sections of the community are all features of such celebratory masking events in Africa.

One of the outstanding features of carnival is the way in which spectators frequently join performers in an informal manner. In many

performances in Africa too, it is both appropriate and desirable that key spectators participate in the performance. In many African performances, it is essential to have certain members of society present among the spectators; elders, senior women, leaders of a specific society. If it is a festival to commemorate the dead, then their family members must occupy a place in the audience at some stage of the proceedings. In carnival too there is a required spectatorship — the figures of authority, important members of the community from the arts, politics and social life. Nor is their presence restricted to observing and viewing, for there are always opportunities to join in at some stage and dance along. ◼

Carlton Garcia

Around carnival time, most Mas men lose their girlfriends or wives. When I say lose, what I mean is, it's a love and everything else is second. You leave home and you might not see them for the next two weeks, you sleep at the Mas camp, you work 'til you get really tired and you're not going home to rest. You find a space under a bench with some foam and you take a rest then get up and when you wake up, you go

again. I had an experience working on a machine, sewing, making costumes and I rested my head on the machine for about half an hour and then wake up and keep going. We have a thing we say, a carnival 'jomby', it's a term we use, like a folk thing. When that carnival 'jomby' hits you, nothing else matters and somehow something always happens with a member of the group. It's not a jinx but something always happens.

Interview

CG Danny Holder   PN Pax Nindi

Danny Holder

ran the route management of Notting Hill Carnival until 2001. This involved scheduling of Mas bands around the route. He started off as a costume maker in 1974 with other young people in the Notting Hill area, including his brother Anton and his sister, Claire Holder who was the Chief Executive of the Carnival. Danny was leader of Ebony Mas Band from 1975-1979 and Executive of the Carnival Arts Committee 1982-89. By profession a computer programmer, Danny is currently co-director of the Carnival Roadshow Company and is touring worldwide.

PN When I spoke with Claire about the origins and history of the Notting Hill Carnival (NHC), I mentioned that I keep meeting people who claim that they are either responsible for its existence or they are an authority on it. I'd like your point of view, as someone who has seen NHC's development from its beginning to this present day.

DH I can give you my perspective, but we'll never all agree on the truth! Some time ago, I was arguing with somebody about my relevance to carnival and they were arguing about their relevance to carnival. We recall things completely differently. I've been involved for nearly 30 years on a serious level and I record things my way.

PN What carnival club were you involved with when you started designing costumes for NHC?

DH We started making costumes for Ebony Steel Band. I was section leader. The production of the costumes, that was myself, my brother and sister and other people in the area. We were just teenagers at the time, but we've stuck with it over the years.

PN Can you tell me your own perspective of how the NHC started?

DH I can only speak from 1971 onwards. In 1971-72, Carnival was very much a local affair, probably no more than about 2-3000 people. There was always a large festival in Powis Square where there would be mostly white people. There was some street activity where we would get any kind of percussion instruments, be it a bin lid, or more conventional instruments like iron, timbale's, going round the streets.

By 1973 Leslie Palmer had taken over the street activity. He did a massive promotion campaign with Capital Radio, which was also launching itself that same year. There was a link between Leslie Palmer's Carnival Committee and Capital Radio that year; they must have sponsored them in some way because they joined the two companies for the specific development and promotion of carnival. Leslie did an amazing job of promoting carnival in London; it grew from local awareness to something massive. I actually have a very vivid images of Leslie walking round the streets in 1973 trying to convince people to make some costumes, or bring a sound system, or join that steel band – you can do it man! Yeah, he and Bigger Hamilton walked the streets and he approached me a number of times to tell me to do something for that year. In those days I must've been 18.

PN So what were you doing at the time yourself?

DH I was a student. I joined Ebony and in those days they were probably no more than three steel bands in the carnival

PN So what were the three bands at the time?

DH Actually there were only two - Metronome and Ebony. The 'London All Stars' came in either 1976 or 1977, so did 'Glissando', and there was a band around at the time called 'Paddington Youth. 1977 was a crucial year. In 1976/77 the riot thing came and things became a lot more radical after that and you got bands like 'Lion Youth' and 'Peoples War' and 'Cocoyea'.

PN How much area did Carnival cover – is it the same route?

DH No, the route came about in the 1980's, people just went around whatever street they fancied because there were no floats in the conventional sense, no tractors to pull anything, just whatever you could carry basically. However, Metronome and Ebony had floats but there were no great hindrances so you could go down any street you felt like going down.

PN So lets get back to making costumes.

DH We made costumes on a community basis – there were about 30-40 of us and we did it as cheaply as possible. Karen Hamilton was central to my section, she was the

only person who was an artist and who had any artistic intention, the rest of us were just workers. Essentially we knew we were capable of industry. As a matter of fact, one of the qualifications for joining my section in Ebony, was that you contributed to making your costume. If you didn't contribute, then you couldn't get one and you couldn't join the section.

PN And was the competition element there at that time?

DH I'm pretty sure it was but it wasn't substantial in the sense that there weren't many bands, there were individuals who brought costumes. At the time there was an organisation that put on a competition that was nothing to do with Carnival directly. Victor Crystal's organisation put on a big show on the Sunday night of Carnival and we would submit the costumes for competition.

PN How did Carnival progress from there?

DH Oh, Carnival developed massively under Leslie Palmer's guidance, it went from strength to strength as new bands came in. People that you had no idea were creative turned up playing steel pans and making costumes. A number of bands grew and grew to the level steady pace that we've got today basically.

PN From your experience, how much difference is there between the costumes you were making in the seventies and the costumes you make now?

DH Great differences. People like me were only holding on until the real artists arrived! I am not an artist, though there are people (like Arthur Peters) who were there then and are still there now. Arthur is an artist who was the shining light of Carnival. He has been right through and makes costumes for Mangrove. Arthur and Lawrence Noel, made costumes for Ebony as well in those days. They've remained pretty constant and are still around. Peter Minshall was in London in the 1970s so we also had that level of costume making. Apart from those central characters, carnival costume makers were not a shadow of what there are today. Today it is a fantastic thing.

PN Did characters like Lawrence Noel and Peter Minshall actually come with their skills from Trinidad or did they learn it in England as they went along?

DH They must've had the artistic instinct; Peter Minshall in particular. I think Lawrence Noel would've come here as a costume maker to make costumes. He must've been a costume maker in the Caribbean before he came here. I would guess that Peter Minshall came here as a student to get qualified in some artistic discipline and happened to end up focusing on carnival costume making.

PN What was your involvement after that?

DH I continued making costumes, but left the country for a few years. I went back to Trinidad and continued to make costumes. In 1982, I came back from Trinidad. I was then on the Carnival committee with Victor Critchlow, Alex Pascall, Norton McLean, Loftas Burton, with Pepe Francis as the worker. I continued in the middle of all that and I started my own band with my partner Keith Lakhan.

PN What was the name of your band?

DH "L & H Wajangs" - we operated it for a couple of years and the theme was "Mops", so basically there was no particular focus on costuming, just going on a lower level kind of tradition of the old Mas - anything goes basically. We would dye mops as many colours as we could to create an impact on the street, but we were good and I think we were the biggest band in NHC for two years. On the route we had international artists such as 'Burning Flames'. One year we had David Rudder and Charlie's Roots, so it was a more dynamic setting or input to Carnival.

PN I would like to go back to confirming any of the old history like Unity and Carnival management.

DH There are some personalities from Unity that got involved in the late eighties. They didn't come as Unity, they came as individuals - Rhodan Gordon and Claire. There was a great tradition of conflicting personalities in the Grove. It was based on long standing grievances between certain characters. The principal characters were Selwyn Baptiste, Darcus Howe, Rhodan Gordon and Granville Price. These

four men had been in conflict and they were all Carnival personalities in the 1970s-1980s. They were in conflict all the time and the conflict radiated right through the entire Carnival management. When Darcus took over carnival between 1977 and 1979, it was a very dynamic time. He was the first person ever to define the responsibilities of the committee, and the power and rights of the committee. He made great political statements in the way that he does. This was probably very good in terms of solidifying the whole Carnival experience. Darcus gave the steel bands, costume makers and the sound system people a perspective on their ownership, which was actually very relevant at the time. Aspects of his perspective, which include artistic representation on the management committee still, follow through to the Carnival today.

PN OK, so apart from the costumes during that period there were also the sound systems, live bands and soca on the move. Which ones contributed towards NHC current musical forms?

DH Collectively they all did. They all went off in their own directions because the steel bands and costume bands greatly resented the sound systems that Leslie Palmer brought in. Whenever anybody from a steel band got up in a meeting they would always complain about the sound systems.

There was also a kind of island identity that went with the music. The sound systems were largely from

the Jamaican community and the steel bands and costume bands were from Trinidad and the smaller islands. By that time, I think the majority of people in Carnival were actually born in England, but they were still holding onto their island identity a generation down the road.

What really changed the face of carnival was the sound systems becoming mobile sound systems, I suppose Lord Sam was the first. So the steel bands and costume bands could no longer complain about the sound systems, simply because they were now having sound systems playing music for them on the streets.

PN How was music presented before that?

DH It was largely steel bands and there were one or two brass bands. There was a band called 'Masquerade' that probably started on the road in the late seventies.

PN What sort of music would they have been playing?

DH Soca, yes and probably fifteen, twenty musicians, they were a big band.

PN That's no longer there is it?

DH No, that has now completely disappeared, though there have been others.

PN What about the live music? I remember there was a time when carnival used to have Arrow and Sparrow coming over?

DH They never really participated in Carnival on the road, Sparrow didn't anyway.

PN Just merely entertaining on the side?

DH Oh no, Sparrow and Arrow had a major record deal and the committee must've paid for him, well, sponsored him to get onto a carnival stage. But there was no great tradition of great artists appearing on the road at all. The Arrow was the first and that was probably in the mid-eighties.

PN Did live appearance by British bands that were commercially successful at the time such as Aswad and Musical Youth help in marketing Carnival?

DH Oh yeah, they certainly did. The live stage concept was Wilf Walker's great project in Carnival, which was developed in 1978. He brought the live stages into Meanwhile Gardens. His two great successes of the time were Musical Youth and Aswad. That actually contributed to the Carnival as a whole and yet had no impact on the traditional elements of Carnival. It was a new dimension in Carnival and a valid one. There were absolutely no connections with what happened on the stage in Meanwhile Gardens, in Portobello Road, Horniman Pleasance and what happened on route, or with steel bands, or pre-carnival events. It's just another facet of Carnival to facilitate other audiences.

PN What were the other music styles found in Carnival apart from Reggae, Soca and Calypso? For example Afrikan music?

DH I can't remember how far back Lord Eric goes in Carnival, but he occasionally comes on the road with his British African (Ghanaian) music – he normally plays in Powis Square. He tends to turn up with various arrangements, but he has been fairly consistent over the last twenty years. He was probably the first instance of music from Africa in Carnival.

PN OK, what is your feeling of Carnival now?

DH It has developed greatly. With the Carnival that went from the 1970s to 1980s there was great institutional conflict in the sense that we got on with nobody. It was difficult for Carnival to negotiate any deals because I got the impression that we were always defined in terms of the conflict level we were in at the time. We were in conflict with the police, the funding bodies, the London Borough Grant schemes, everybody. So it had been a difficult time leading up until I would say recently.

There was a case in 1988 when a lot of people were raided and arrested for fraud investigations. I myself was interviewed for nine hours by the police. In their investigations they said they had assigned 47 members of the Serious Fraud Office to investigate Carnivals' affairs and they confiscated every single piece of paper from the Carnival office in one of their dawn raids and they found nothing, or nothing of any substance.

PN So at that time what was your responsibilities with Carnival?

DH I was on the committee, there was a board of directors at the time, and we were going through exactly the same phase as Carnival is going through now – the transition between being a commercial company to a charity. I was on the board of Directors, there were five of us: myself, Alex Pascall, Norton McLean, Joyce Bacchus and Victor Critchlow. I was in charge of live stages and stalls.

PN Did carnivalists feel like the raids were very much like the police trying to say, take it easy with Carnival?

DH Well, I think because of the way Carnival emerged out of the community, there's always a lot of frustration. There was no possible income base for anybody so by and large people were always accusing each other of stealing money. I'm not saying that there were grounds for the police to take up one of these whispers and raid someone's house. They definitely exploited the atmosphere created in the Carnival community - that everybody was building swimming pools and building houses in the Caribbean with carnival money. The police were able to use this mistrust as reasons for raiding us and changing our structure.

PN Now things have changed, is it more like working in partnerships and collaboration with the police, the council, funding bodies?

DH Oh yes, very much. But there is still a struggle going on. However, the relationship between the Carnival and various authorities is actually workable, whereas in the 1970s and 1980s it was not workable, there were two conflicting objectives really.

PN Some people say that the relationships with authorities ruins the anarchy of Carnival, and others say that relationship makes a safe environment to be working with.

DH People say that, I was listening to a radio broadcast by a Daily Mail black reporter Baz Bamigboye, a Nigerian guy I think. He was quoted as saying that Carnival is now boring, it's too well organised. That's the image I think people want to relate to the danger although it's detrimental to the black community. It gives the impression that we can't relate to institutions and we can't structure ourselves in terms of a working organisation. People still want the anarchy and the suspicion and the conflict – even someone like Baz Bamigboye who's a journalist or a feature writer of a National newspaper. He might say it's too well organised for him but he's taking a back seat. I suppose a lot of people do use Carnival as a band wagon. People like to say they are associated with Carnival and they can make statements about it because people have traditionally never sued anybody for saying that Carnival is what it isn't, or isn't what it is.

PN What about culture? In the past carnival has been pigeon holed as a black thing or would you say this has changed?

DH It is a black thing, but it does require very main stream, structured facilitation. The artistic development of Carnival is today a black development. It does go in black directions probably largely reinforced by the Caribbean experience in the first instance and then now largely the British black experience. It is a black thing and it has every right to be a black thing and it is the shining example of black achievement in Britain. I can't think of a bigger or better black achievement in this country than the NHC.

PN I have heard different versions of stories relating to some of the committees that were involved in the past. Their structures and chairs, for example, the Carnival Arts Committee and the Carnival Development Committee. What is your knowledge on this part of the history of the management of Carnival and was it as controversial as the media made people to believe?

DH Leslie Palmer left the Carnival directly after the riots and got a job with Island records and moved on. The Carnival committee split themselves into two. Louis Chase went in one direction with the Carnival Arts Committee (CAC). Selwyn and Darcus went in another direction with the Carnival Development Committee (CDC). For a while Darcus managed to get all the bands signed up to the CDC. But Louis Chase was an institutional figure, he's a black guy from the Notting Hill area. So, although there were no bands signed to the CAC, they were actually still funded by, the Arts Council, as well as the CRE.

Louis Chase became the chairman of the CAC and Darcus became the chairman of the CDC. In the newspapers and on the TV, Carnival was reported in terms of these two committees fighting each other for institutional money. That went on for a while, although Louis Chase's CAC only had stewards in Carnival. Darcus' committee had all the bands and all the sound systems, so it worked in that kind of way. So one committee had all the stewards and the other had all the bands.

Because of infighting, the CDC collapsed in 1980. Then all the bands moved over to the CAC in 1981. Now the CAC had inherited the stewards and all the bands. So, it's probably since 1981 that has been this one committee concept, but prior to that there had been conflict and a lot of bad press.

VJ Ramlal got involved in a bank story that brought Carnival into disrepute. One day him and a colleague went to pay in some money into the bank and the girl stamped the receipt before taking the money. They thought 'Oh my Goodness, here's a chance to make some personal money', ran off with the money claiming they'd paid it in as they had the stamp receipt. Then the bank worked it out and they got charged. That was actually the one major Carnival fraud story in the history of Carnival – that's the big one! I think there was about two to three thousands pounds involved. Scandalous! Shameful!

Junior Telfer was also reasonably constant between Leslie Palmer's committee and Louis Chase's. He was one of the great public speakers, he was around with Michael X. He was a Trinidadian and a Syrian – wore a turban, cut a dash and was a major personality of the area. He was one of the characters who floated around Carnival negotiating deals and creating an image for the committee as he was quite a glamorous personality. Frank Bynoe had been part of the committee with Victor Critchlow and they did the commercial activity that staged the costume competition in Hammersmith Palais every year. That was the days before there was any Carnival competition, so they basically contributed to the Carnival in that way.

PN What did you do in terms of the promotion company you had and who were the acts?

DH My partner Keith Lakhan and I had L&H Calypso Promotions and were probably the first touring circuit. Over the years 1981-1993 we toured Soca acts and calypso shows from the Caribbean in and around Britain. We would do three nights at the Shaw Theatre on Euston Road and extend them into a ten-date tour. We would do major outdoor events, either at Wormwood Scrubs, or stadiums in North London. We did as many as 25 shows a year featuring international artists from the Caribbean. We were able to put artists on the road. That's how we managed to start all those mops bands on the road.

PN What about the likes of Lee Jasper, what was his involvement in carnival?

had promised us funding for a tent in 1988 and then later withdrew the offer. It was complicated by the fact that we had plans to sublet the tent. We even had people to hire it. But the LBGS withdrew the funding at the last minute. We financially collapsed in 1988. We owed lots of people money including the costume bands and steel bands. The stewards actually rioted and made sure they got paid. We left owing the stage building company money for the live stages and the tent. It was difficult in 1988.

PN So how did carnival go around cleaning up the debts?

DH Oh that's how Claire came in, Claire represented firmer business. So she basically disbanded the committee and set up a new one without inheriting the debts of the old committee.

PN So who runs the Carnival today? What do you think about people asking this question and why do people ask this question?

DH Well, Carnival is a collaboration. It has actually emerged from the 1970s as a collaboration of disciplines and culture. Claire and her Carnival office executed Carnival policy and did it very well. However, I think that most of the disciplines of Carnival get a fair shake on the day and they couldn't do this unless there was some input by them into the running of Carnival. So, it's a collaboration of the various disciplines that run Carnival really but they do come out of the artistic content of Carnival.

DH Lee was never really involved in carnival, he was elected one year in 1989 along with myself and Claire, but Claire disbanded that committee and formed the new one.

PN So that's how the next one came about

DH Yes, we were all in court because the London Borough Grants Scheme

Call and Response; Commentary and Scandal
– Calypso in Carnival

Alexander Kelly
Loewenthal
(aka Alexander D. Great)

bands were often augmented by clarinet or violin. The modern calypso tents are large halls seating over a thousand people and carrying groups with as many as fifteen musicians, including a large brass and percussion section. Calypso tents are well attended during the carnival season. Here the public can get to the nitty-gritty of political and social matters.

Initially, lyrics were the premier consideration of calypsonians. From the middle of the nineteenth until the first quarter of the twentieth century, the majority of kaisos were sung to stock melodies, mostly in the minor mode and generally of eight-line stanzas. With a few notable exceptions, it is not until the 1940's and 1950's that we hear any ground-breaking experiments in melodic writing, mainly from Atilla The Hun, Kitchener and Mighty Sparrow. Indeed, Atilla (Raymond Quevedo) has given a superb description of kaiso. He says kaiso is not a melody and words strung together to picture a particular idea but the "cohesion of several interconnected parts manifesting themselves in a single work of art calculated to completely satisfy the meticulously fastidious demands of its worshipping votaries". A very calypsonian description!

In spite of living in the age of multi-media, the power of words and music delivered with wit and irony still holds enormous sway in the essentially oral culture of the Caribbean. The calypsonian's voice is the voice of the people and great exponents of the art invariably bring politics, social issues, scandal and

world topics to the carnival stage. At one time the true test of a great calypsonian was their ability to improvise lyrics on the spot and this is still preserved in the 'Extempo' competition held every year in Trinidad. Two calypsonians will sing alternate verses in a war of insults known as 'picong' (from the French piquant) and the first to hesitate or not make a verse with the required rhyme or syllabic scan is the loser.

In the past, there were occasions when the tent performers skills in improvisation were tested on the spot, usually precipitated by some noteworthy visitor. On such occasions all the members of the tent would be expected to make up a verse immediately (hence the usefulness of stock melodies). One highly acclaimed kaisonian of the 1920s, The Inventor (Henry Forbes) was wont to lambast his compatriots in song if he felt their contribution fell short of the mark. On one particular day, the tent was visited by Councillor Bodu - one of society's elite who supported kaiso. The Inventor decided that one of his fellow performers was below par. The unlucky recipient of his disgust was treated to the following extempore observation:

"I intended to give you a castigation
But instead you will get my compassion
You have demonstrated your inability
And you have failed miserably
You can't sing on Papa Bodu whom we all know
The friend and patron of caliso (kaiso)
You can't give satisfaction
You are a mock calypsonian."

Essentially the calypsonian draws his or her inspiration from topics that have caught the imagination of the greater populace during the previous year. Scandal and vulgarity were always safe bets, but the way to the people's hearts, as many top performers found, was through the lampooning and chastising of authority.

Down the years, there have been many popular calypso talents, even so, some stand out as giants of the form.

King Radio (Norman Span) a waterfront worker in Port of Spain was a real people's calypsonian. With no pretensions to lofty ideals or language he sang songs of sexual innuendo and occasionally complained of authority. In 1933 he sang "Country Club Scandal" about a high-ranking police officer and a white woman, which immediately thrust him into the limelight with the upper strata of society. They, more than anyone, loved to hear their peers discomfited by calypso's double-entendre. In 1937, in response to the banning of labour leader Uriah Butler from going about his normal business he admonished the government with;

"They want to licence me mout',
they don't want me to talk
They want to licence me foot, they don't want me to walk."

His most famous song, "Matilda" was Road March for three years running, 1938-40 and deals with his favourite topic, the fickleness of woman.

"Matilda, Matilda, Matilda she take me money and gone Venezuela."

The majority of the common people laid the blame for their living and working conditions on the government, the police or (as they saw it) foreign invaders in the form of the American forces. These themes recur time and again. In 1943 Lord Invader brought to the carnival one of the greatest calypso hits of all time, "Rum and Coca-Cola". Invader bemoans the state of immorality then rife in Trinidad that he sees as a direct result of the American presence on the island. The first verse sets the scene.

"Since the Yankees came to Trinidad - They have the young girls going mad. The girls they say treat them nice - And they give them a better price."

The Mighty Sparrow made his mark in 1956 with the first of a series of calypsos which have made him undisputed King for the past forty years. "Jean and Dinah", probably his most famous song, dealt with "the Yankees" again but this time in jubilation at their leaving the island. Sparrow gloats in the certain knowledge that:

"Jean and Dinah, Rosita and Clementina
On the corner posing, bet your life it's something they selling
If you catch them broke you can get them all for nothing
Don't make a row, the Yankees gone, Sparrow take over now."

Sparrow has used his voice, melody

and wit to sway opinion in all sorts of ways. When in the 1960s the government, led by Dr. Eric Williams, introduced the P.A.Y.E. tax system Sparrow anticipated the general mood of resistance in the populace and set out to educate them.

"The doctor say to pay as you earn
Sparrow say you paying to learn
M'father say he sharpening the axe
for when the collector come to chip
off the income tax."

Having explained to his listeners the need for the new taxation system Sparrow gives the twist in the last line of the song -

"M'father say he selling the axe
for when the collector come
to pay off the income tax."

Sparrow's only real rival for the top spot is Calypso's Grand Master, Lord Kitchener who died in February 2000. He took steel pan composition to its peak. He spent some time in Britain, arriving on the H.M.S. Windrush in 1948 and remaining until 1962. In Britain he popularised calypso to a great extent whilst at the same time taking on board the sophisticated night club arrangements of the band at the Cafe de Paris in London where he often worked. These influences show in his chord progressions and melodic lines, which are unsurpassed in their elegance and poise. He has also pioneered a song structure consisting of Verse, bridge, false chorus - real chorus, wherein he sets up the tune in such a way that when the listener feels that they

have reached the chorus in fact there is another section of music to come. We know when we have reached the real chorus because a 'call and response' figure is offered to the audience in which they can participate. Kitchener had to reduce the structure of his songs back to three sections because he felt the steel bands occasionally found the complexities beyond them. Among his best kaisos are "Pan in A Minor", "Mystery Band", "Earthquake" and "Heavy Roller" - all songs extolling the pan. Kitchener was as prolific as Sparrow and his genius is sorely missed.

The 1970s saw the advent of soca, a mix of soul and calypso. The greater part of the calypso message stayed the same but soca brought with it some dilution of topicality, political statement and protest. Soca concerns itself more with party than politics. However, some of the best modern calypso singers call themselves soca artists whilst maintaining all the best traditions of kaiso. These are David Rudder, one of the most daring and experimental, Shadow, Black Stalin, Gypsy and The Mighty Chalkdust. Gipsy won the 1997 contest with a song entitled "little Black Boy" dealing with the street urchins and their plight in the capital.

Shadow is graphic in his declamatory style. Most of his calypsos have a social message or lesson to convey. "Survival Business", one of his most striking, is blunt and to the point.

"Survival Business - is a crucial business

Survival Business - is a brutal business.
The cat loves the rat - but the rat don't need a love like that,
He loves the rat for his face - he love the way rat face does taste."

David Rudder, always searching for new modes of expression in Kaiso brought a masterpiece of simplicity and invention to the carnival in 1998. "High Mas'" caused controversy among Trinidad's more pious Christians by dealing with the subject of Carnival as though it were a High Mass in church. He asks God to

"Forgive us this day our daily weakness as we cast our mortal burden on your city"

all chanted in an ecclesiastical monotone. The crowd's response is "Amen". He then asks God to

"send us a little Soca for some healing"

and so the song progresses. Certain press reports claimed that it was sinful to ask for forgiveness for a pre-meditated transgression i.e. to "get on bad" at Carnival.

There is also a whole new wave of young Caribbean artists who are mixing different styles and genres to create new ways of conveying the Kaiso message. Karene Asche, fourteen year old Junior Calypso Monarch of Trinidad for 1998, won with a song entitled "since you've been gone", not a lover's lament but a cry to absent fathers to think about their responsibilities.

Wherever carnival is celebrated calypso will be found. The huge variety of dance music styles now being created, from R'n'B through reggae and dancehall to drum 'n' bass all have their roots in calypso. Social commentary is alive and well at carnival and the continuing role of the calypsonian is ensured whatever the musical label.

Arthur France Leeds Carnival

The first year of Carnival in Leeds, 1967, stands out for me as the best year. Most people never believed it would happen. Everyone pulled the idea to bits, "It's a bad idea", "It's nonsense, just something for white people to laugh at". But as long as you have support from a few, nothing is impossible.

I knew my rights and we had a right to perform and do our thing so I went ahead and organised the Carnival, the police and the park. Two people in particular, Willie Robertson and Calvin Beach were very enthusiastic and supportive. We made five Queen costumes within a week. We also formed a steel band. I must admit I'm very much in love with steel band music. I was in touch with some people in Birmingham so I was able to influence them and they also brought some costumes over. We wanted to involve the newscaster Calvin Allen so we contacted him on the phone and found out that he was so enthusiastic about it.

We had a calypso competition. The first black matron in England, Daphne Steel, was invited, and we had the manager of the Leeds City Town Hall. The Hall was packed the first night of the Queens' Show. I think people had come to laugh at us, they didn't expect to see something like this. When Clive Allen turned up it was so exciting to see him in person. When the curtain was drawn, he stood on stage to make the announcements and people were gobsmacked. He was brilliant, his voice and his charisma.

When the costumes came out, they couldn't believe it, they didn't expect to see anything like that. It was extremely exciting, fifteen thousand people had turned up from Leeds, Birmingham, Manchester and the surrounding area. Being black, people didn't believe we could start things and keep them going, yet we can keep things going, for as long as it takes. Carnival is the only event that brings so many people together, from all around the country, all around the world.

ON ROUTE

View from the Top

Monica
Rene

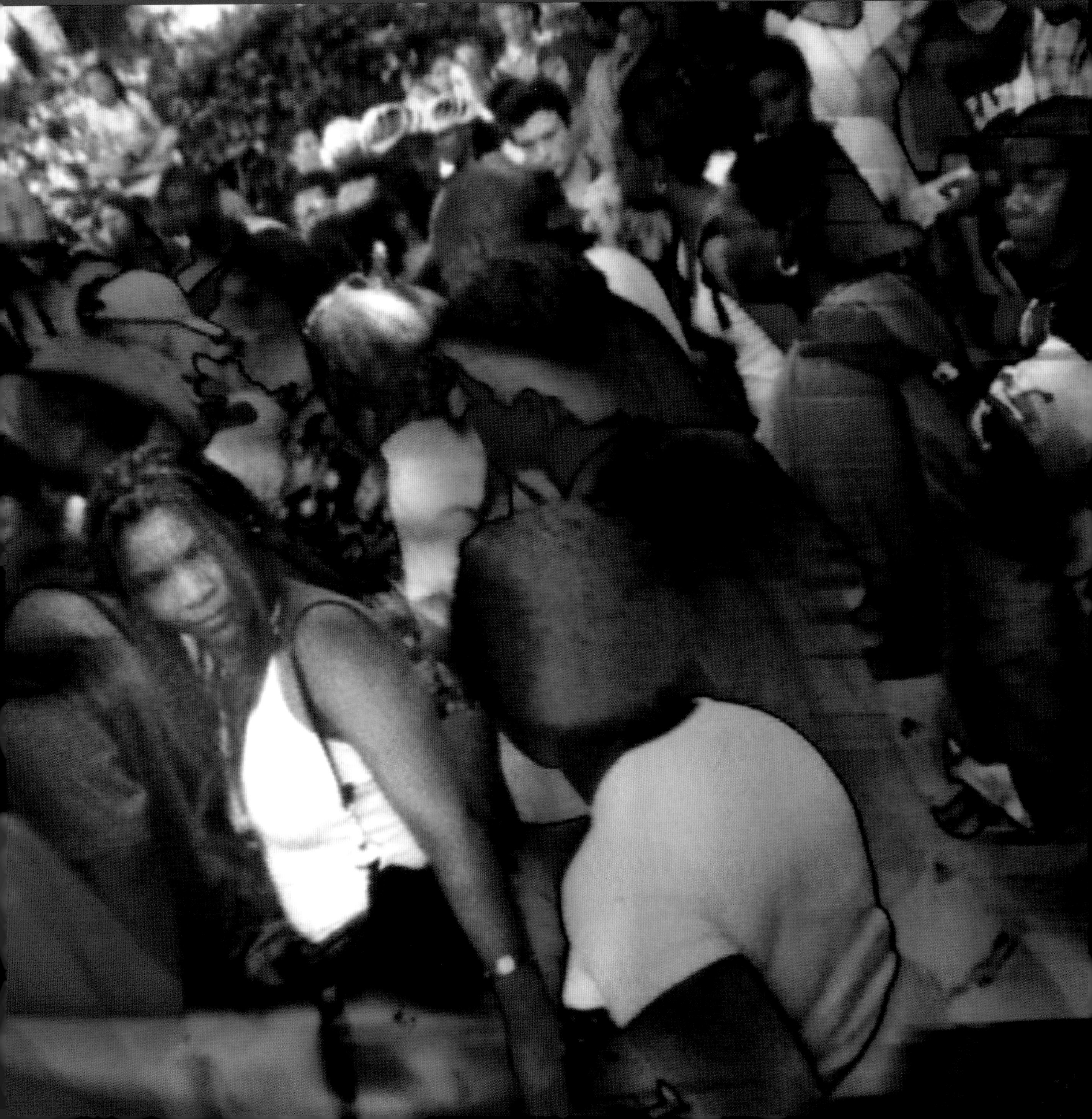

Most of us living in the area of the Notting Hill Carnival consider this big event to be cultural and social education.

Monica René

was born in Jamaica and educated in Oxford, England. She worked as an international fashion model and journalist before pursuing her interest in art and culture. She has spent time in Egypt and the USA while researching a Phd at London University. Monica also holds a BA Hons in Film, Video and Photographic Arts, and an MA in Art History.

Each year British "multi-culturalness" is so evident. Although the originators of the Notting Hill Carnival were West Indians, the effect the event has on British "Afro-Caribbean-ness" is astounding and most black families find it a very important part of showing their young ones the importance of maintaining this event. The varied themes in carnival arts testify to many traditional attachments and most emphasise values that one would generally categorise in a cultural context as religious, political and/or sexual. These brought to the forefront through this event place emphasis on our cultural diversity. Race mixing goes much further than the obvious and the products of these multi-cultural unions are inspired to create relationships that become rich with references that will fire many their ideas for events such as Carnival.

For me, the past 16 years of living on route has seen waves of mega-excitement and great reunions. Friends and acquaintances from diverse places turn up on my doorstep, some only by sheer coincidence, because they know my house is always open to them for the two days. Although my sense of cultural, social and community responsibilities are heightened at this particular time each year, Carnival brings great stress and excitement in a twin package. If one gets ill, for example, getting medical attention can be problematic and although I have seen ambulances parked in nearby streets the multitude dancing and moving at a slow pace create pockets of body jam which to the sick trying to get out can be very frightening. If for example, one is in a sickle-cell crisis or an epileptic fit, the street party can be almost fatal, so in my opinion there should be safe areas allocated to the sick and some disabled enclaves along the route. Many elderly people live alone in my neighbourhood and some are unsettled by the trouble Carnival causes. In general it is very difficult for them to get out and unfortunately, in this case, our area of Ladbroke Grove is one where such body massing occurs so viewing it can be worrying for some. The lengthy street parties with ongoing noise late into the night also disturb our normally calm vicinity. Although the police gets the 'mas' out at reasonable times, during Carnival week-end it is not unusual to hear well controlled middle-class residents angrily opening windows at ungodly hours of the night to shout, "I am **** trying to ***** sleep - turn the ******music down". Of course the party throwers and goers can't hear a thing, not even the police knocking down their doors. Complaints get forgotten when morning arrives and as the day of Carnival begins the neighbourhood is happy again.

Aspects of our African, European and Caribbean cultural heritage will always be present wherever we live, but at Carnival there is a consistent effort always to

unite culturally in having a great festivity. Our food, music and art can get open acknowledgement, but with the stereotypical violence we need to unite against thugs, bully boys, hooliganism, and ruffians. After all, embracing our varied historical and cultural backgrounds can and should only lead to the uplift of generations to come. Most of us born in the Caribbean, now living in the UK, feel that we record our journey through these corridors of carnival, but too often violence drops in a nasty blot to unfortunately make 'good' media headlines.

The Notting Hill Carnival route includes a sizeable part of the street Ladbroke Grove. I live on Ladbroke Grove. This provides a very privileged view of the annual celebrations and I do consider myself to be in an advantageous situation to watch the parade from my home. Sitting at the kitchen window with all my cameras, films and lenses to hand I manage to photograph many things of interest as well as carnival costumes and bands. I often leave my window seat to run down the stairs into the parade to get a better shot. But running in and out of the masquerade can be quite difficult. Not only do I have to push through the throngs of people crowding my doorstep, but getting from sidewalk to street involves much negotiating, as standing spots are fiercely guarded especially when a band is in procession.

Most bands are familiar with my rushing into their enclosure, pointing my camera, dancing along with them, taking my shots and leaving, I have done it for years and some really don't mind. Both overhead and ground level shots are useful as all bands parade in front of my door during Carnival days. As such, I consider my work a to be a "cultural documentarist". The procession generally moves slower as it approaches my end of Ladbroke Grove towards the station, affording me time to really take in the themes and music of each parading band. There is always a crowd on the corners of Cambridge & Oxford Gardens as some costumed bands enter the procession from these nearby streets. From my window I see the excitement they create for the crowd who jump in exhilaration on each entrance.

One Sunday morning at six thirty my doorbell rang. I dragged myself out of bed to answer a visitor from Birmingham asking to set up food stall on my doorstep. I had to refuse when shouts from the bedroom interrupted the bell noise with, "Who the hell can this be ringing down my doorbell so early on Sunday morning. Tell them to push off!" "Its a visitor from country wanting to book a space on our doorstep for his ageing mother to view the procession!", answered I, telling a white lie. The family eventually found a spot for a food stall a few doors down while they kept an eye on grandma who took up my offer of a chair on the doorstep from 11.30am to 6.30pm.

Another year a group of people asked the neighbours across the road for a doorstep stall space. The table stacked with pots and containers ready to sell prided delicacies among the bulk of carnival attractions was suddenly disarranged by the screaming sounds of fire engines and police car sirens deafening the area. Ladbroke Grove was cleared at high speed and directly across from my home water spewed and spouted up above the houses and tree-tops flooding the street all the way to the tube station. Ackee and saltfish, bread, roti, curried goat and jerk chicken floated with price tags, corn on the cob amidst charcoal and rice and peas, down the street in their own individual parade. This emergency created by a faulty gas cylinder, used to warm up the stall's food, had helicopters hovering overhead as the Met men moved at break-neck speed to clear the incoming crowd. While ambulances drew close to fire engines for unseen emergencies, the cylinder cooled from its excitement was taken away from the revelry. Punch bowls re-emerged from safe crowded living rooms and balconies, roof tops, window sills and doorsteps became occupied again to welcome the street party. A few minutes later the sound systems buzzed the inflowing crowd into the dance and the procession flowed down Ladbroke Grove without anyone noticing the wetness of this particular stretch... Since that year all food stalls are safely put into areas allocated by the Carnival Office.

Carnival in Rio is world renowned as is the Carnival in Trinidad but the unique blend of Notting Hill has fired the idea of the street party into another dimension. Some musicians often come together to play drums indoors, but since Brazilian music hit our streets they now enter the procession often after sitting atop gate posts awaiting the rhythms of the Brazilian bands. On my bit of the Grove, they follow the band sometimes just to the Ladbroke Grove Bridge beating their drums or whatever they can find to the Samba 'riddim'. My party generally joins in all shouting and jumping up with noises like 'Hot! Hot! Hot!' and dance frenziedly to this 'traditional' carnival heat. Samba rhythm is a great addition to Notting Hill Carnival. Calypso, steel pan, reggae rock, soca music etc. have definitely captured our hip movements in their heyday at street dances, clubs and dark 'shubeens'. House parties throbbed to their lyrics in stuffy atmospheres perfumed with 'curry goat' and beer, while couples locked in close embraces slowly moved to music that kept them on the same spot all night. Samba is not 'rent a tile' music and its liveliness drives a rhythm that even a cripple will shake to. Once I saw a disabled person dressed in a fantastic winged costume dancing frenziedly whirling and turning in his wheelchair down Ladbroke Grove. As he followed the music, many people moved aside to watch him. He was fantastically able to co-ordinate costume and dance with machinery. ▪

Alex Herbert Leeds Carnival

My parents are religious people and they did not approve of things like carnival. I remember when I was nine or ten years old in St. Kitts, my mother went to town and bought a new dress to wear in church. When I saw it, I thought it was wonderful and said so, but my father said it was too beautiful to wear in church. He did not want her to wear the dress, so my mother and father got into an argument about it.

I took the dress and went away with it. I got some scissors and cut it into ribbons. We didn't really have a carnival, but at Christmas the bands would go around in a kind of festival. We would take fig leaves and put them in the sun to dry, stick them onto material and if they were very dry we would paint them different colours. We would take bottle stops, flatten them, put holes in them and put four or five of them on one piece of thread. That was our costume.

Five friends and myself had a piece of my mother's dress, and we went around during the festival getting money. When my Dad found out what I had been doing he beat me three times. I have never had such a beating. I ran to my mother and she hit me too for cutting her dress.

Photographing Carnival – Catching the Spirit

Jacob **Ross**

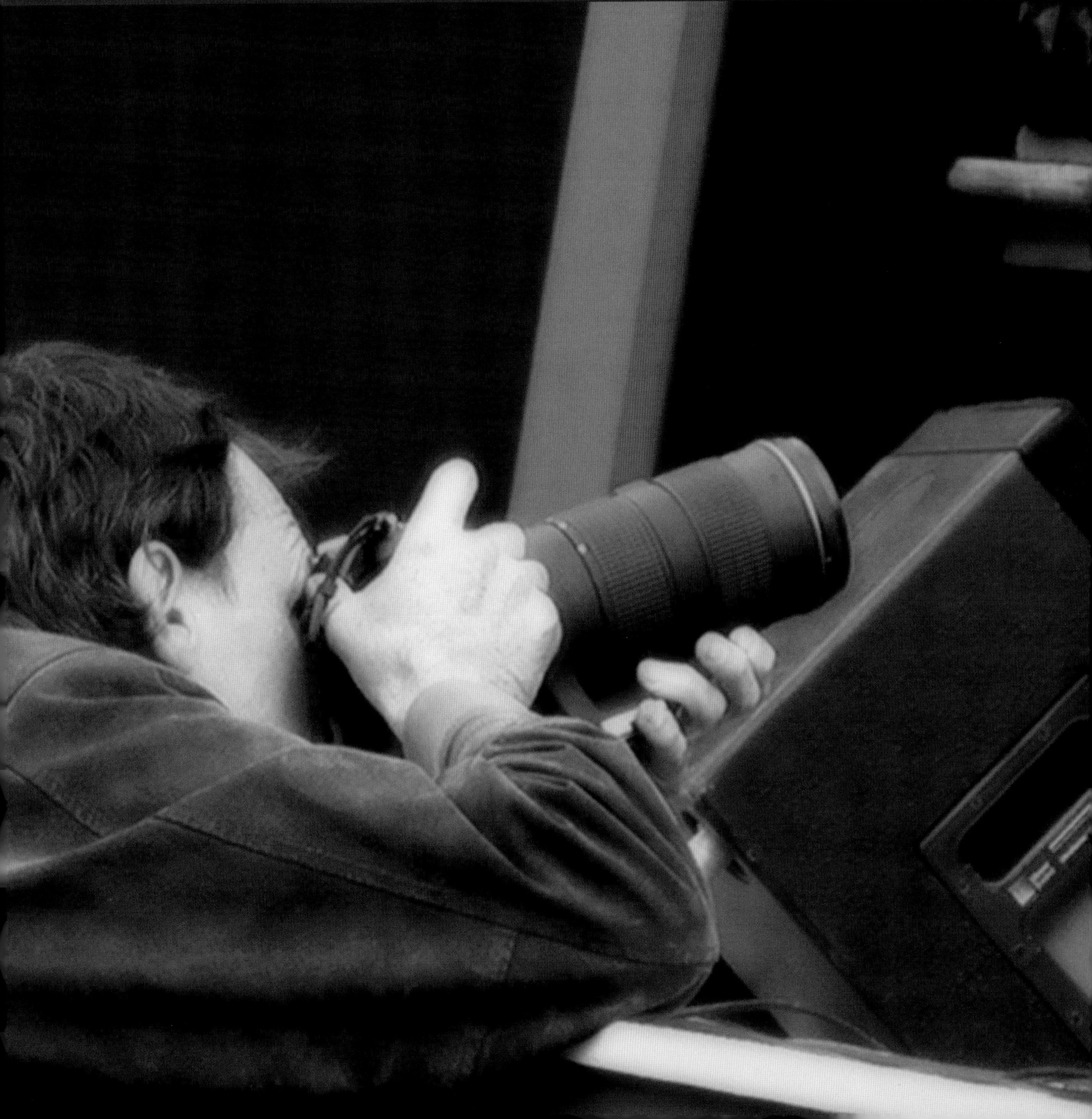

A favourite memory of my early years as a carnival photographer in England was when I climbed a lamppost, secured myself up there with a large leather belt and began to take pictures of Carnival.

Jacob Ross

was born in Grenada and studied at the University of Grenoble, France. He has been residing in Britain since 1984. He is a poet, playwright, journalist, novelist and creative writing tutor. He was formerly an Editor of Artrage Intercultural Arts magazine, Britain's leading Intercultural Arts magazine. He has published two collections of short stories: 'Song for Simone' and 'A Way to Catch the Dust'. And co-authored, 'Behind the Masquerade, the Story of Notting Hill Carnival' with Kwesi Owusu.

A couple of minutes later a photographer on the ground drew the attention of three policemen to my presence on the lamppost. Soon they were gathered below me ordering me to get down. One of them was so concerned about my health and safety he threatened to 'tap' me over the head if I didn't obey promptly. After ten minutes or so of claiming to be stuck while snapping away, common sense told me that I had pushed it as far as I could without getting arrested. I climbed down and in as excited a voice as I could muster I told them of the great view there was from up there. At least one of the three was interested enough to look speculatively up at the post and ask me "Really?"

I remember the incident because of the irony, the possibilities of tension that seem to reside just under the surface of events like Carnival and the way we as photographers have learned to negotiate space and opportunities within the event, in a society that has come to regard any sort of letting go, or risk-taking, as potentially criminal.

I began my acquaintance with photography in the French 'border city' of Grenoble located just under the Alps. I was a student then and very much an alien in a place where, at the time, a black English-speaking male from the Caribbean was more than a rarity. It was the first time I ever owned a camera, or indeed used one. But my introduction to photography, especially Carnival and its possibilities, began much earlier. I was one of those pupils who preferred to do anything else but homework. The library was not so much a source of preparation as a place where I could look and marvel at pictures of other people in other worlds. Photographs were imaginative trampolines that allowed me the opportunity to mind leap into foreign territories and make myself a sort of citizen there until the library closed. National Geographic was especially good at that. And I suppose that it was from there that I began to appreciate 'quality' photography. But these had their value simply because they had no real connection with the Caribbean, or with anything that I could vaguely call familiar.

The shift occurred when I picked up, again in a studious attempt at avoidance, an issue of the Trinidad Guardian newspaper that, as usual, provided extensive coverage of the Trinidad Carnival. You simply looked at the pictures and with a mixture of resentment and awe deplored the fact that their Carnival was so much more spectacular, so much more beautiful than Grenada's. But this

particular issue was different. Except for the obligatory display of the winning bands, and the various kings and queens, there were hardly any photographs of costumes (stunning or otherwise) in the paper. There was, however, a series of photographs of a girl, perhaps fifteen or sixteen years old, taking her very first, tentative steps out into the streets. The camera followed her right through to the final minute of the second day of the event. It had to have taken an inspired photographer to come up with the simple idea of dedicating his entire stock of film over those two days (filled as they are with fights, scandal, drama, and all sorts of improbabilities, and mind-blowing colours and constructions) to concentrate through a telephoto lens, on nothing but a young girl's face.

It was simply awesome, the range of emotions that teenager displayed: the sobriety, the ecstasy, the dignity, the anticipation, the uncaring, the outrage, even the tears as she lived out (one can only speculate here) her own personal dramas within the crucible of one of the great dramas of the twentieth century. It still remains the most poignant photographic essay on carnival that I have ever seen.

What I realised later was that photographers bring their own personalities, ideologies and agendas to the taking of pictures. I have argued elsewhere that differences in culture can and do influence what people choose to photograph, i.e. what they believe is worth photographing. I would even dare to suggest that cultural differences can inform the choices photographers make about the use of a particular lens or focal length over another, and the positions or locations they may decide to photograph from. It is by no means scientific but it is a conclusion I came to after spending a lot of time studying the pictures of many countries by local photographers and those of 'visitors'.

I also confirmed this when I began photographing Carnival in England. Arriving here in the mid 1980s was very much like stepping back a century or two in that the struggles that Caribbean people were experiencing here - largely against the establishment - to hold onto Carnival, to develop it, to go on owning it, to have it in a place and space that had some meaning for them (tied up as it was with their experiences and history of settlement in this country) had already been fought in the Caribbean against colonial and post-colonial religious institutions and governments. We had already had our riots, and 'battle royals' with the police, that is until the event became sanitised and its commercial possibilities recognised and exploited by the very people who were against it in the first case.

I began photographing at the height of the battle to keep Carnival on the streets, or just to keep Carnival. At the time, a significant number of people was convinced that the event would be killed off, or that it would be so modified that it would no longer be worth holding on to.

The police and the national press were ranged against us (by then it had become personal), and the politicians, if they were not condemning the event, were either conspicuously silent or, as one of them admitted later, disinclining to get involved.

One had a sense that more was at stake than simply the dancing and music in the streets. That what it amounted to was a very profound 'dissing' of an essential part of what defined us, an attack against the culture and the history that we came from, and which have been so fundamental to our survival as a people. Interestingly, many West Africans felt just as strongly since, as far as they were concerned the message had wider implications for all Africa-related black people in England.

Photography therefore became part of the argument for Carnival that was coming at the time from a multiplicity of relatively small but very dynamic sources, including publications like Caribbean Times, The Voice, Black Arts in London, Artrage Intercultural Arts Magazine, and a relatively influential left-of-centre London listings magazine called City Limits.

I sought to offer photographs to the people and publications that made it their concern to defend or promote the event. I sought to extract from amongst that mass of moving dancing bodies and costumes, something of the dignity and ingenuity that went into creating the event.

I worked thematically since I soon discovered that for large, 'amorphous' events, where there is no single narrative, where so much is going on at the same time, it pays to work thematically. Carnival is much more of a mass event than, say football or athletics where the individual or group of individuals that the photographer has to focus on is obvious.

My first year, 1986, I concentrated on costumes, the very architecture and the skills involved in making them. I sought to capture and convey through 35mm slides, something of the intention behind these creations. In the process I learnt how designers worked, their remarkable understanding of the human form, the way it moves and how best to distribute the weight of a costume ten to fifteen times a person's size without hampering mobility. Their knowledge of fabric and their properties is often stunning and like any decent photographer they anticipate light and its possible effect on their creation.

Photographing carnival also meant keeping abreast of the developments in film technology. One of the favourite sayings of a photographer friend of mine was that when Kodak made film they didn't have black people in mind far less carnival, the exception being their highly specialised Kodachromes. But who wanted to wait a couple of weeks for pictures to come back? Many of us turned to Japanese stock in order to capture the colour saturation and detail representative of carnival.

The second year, I concentrated on the preparation by masqueraders.

The actual work behind the scenes: the organisation and task-sharing that go towards realising such a large event, the lifestyle and the culture within the workshop itself. In other words the very core of the creativity that we admire so much on our streets. That series confirmed for me that the build-up before Carnival is not just about the making of costumes, it is also a series of carefully co-ordinated rituals and procedures geared at putting the body and the mind into a place of real abandon; of truly letting go. It even extends to the dancehall, especially the month or two leading up to the event - an aspect of Carnival that is so effectively captured in the photographs of Danijah Tafari (Fitzroy Sang).

Another year, I simply focused on people relating to each other: the dynamics between individuals meeting and engaging at the event, since Carnival is largely about that. In 1989 I kept my camera on the children: the lost ones, those perched like little, wonder-struck (or bored) Buddhas on their parents' shoulders, and those you sometimes caught looking on with a complete sense of isolation from the windows of the surrounding buildings. And of course there was the attempt to record the 'multi-culturalisation' of the event, especially in the 1990s with the increasing participation of Indian, Chinese and white European masqueraders.

Youth culture was particularly fascinating because it contained so many strands: sound systems, hair and dress styles, postures and gestures and an energetic will to rave. The buzzword then was attitude, and one found plenty of that there.

The advice I still give to photographers who ask, is to shoot a lot of film. Spend some time selecting the best shots i.e. those that represent what they actually felt and saw and try to improve on that next time. Then destroy the rest. Part of one's responsibility to one's self-development is to examine very critically, the results of a day's shoot. My approach is to discard the ones I don't like even if the exposure might be perfect. Photographers who are familiar with their equipment can readily identify which lens they used, which film stock, as well as the distance and perspective from which they were shooting.

For instance I learnt pretty quickly that working with a moderately wide-angle lens (28mm, 35mm) close up captured a sense of involvement and being 'in there' that I could not obtain with a telephoto lens, since the former introduces just the amount of exaggeration that presents Carnival as it really is experienced, i.e. its spectacular, larger-than-life character.

Carnival is also an excellent training ground for learning to anticipate and 'grab' people at the height of physical expression, since we are talking here about jumping, jostling and swirling targets who really don't care whether you are there or dead. This was the experience that prepared me for example for photographing the Burundi Drummers in full flight, or

Adzido Pan African Dance Ensemble in difficult lighting situations on stage.

The year I decided to give it up and move on to something else was when it seemed more or less confirmed that Carnival was here to stay, at least for a while yet. That was 1993 and the theme I worked with was simply 'confrontation.' Confrontation of any kind really: women hauling up their men for some excess, young women giving over-zealous males the 'back-off' glare, black men negotiating their way through barricades of police or groping for some definition of their manhood through confronting each other.

It was the year also that photography presented me with a real dilemma. I remember my attention being drawn to a small crowd of youths in heated argument over something. And much as a chronic smoker would reach for a cigarette and place it between the lips, I lifted my camera and began taking shots. In a couple of minutes it was over. A white youth was lying on the ground and several others were quickly merging into the crowd. And I had it all on film.

These, sadly, are the kinds of images that sell. One didn't have to be prophetic to see the headlines the next day, or the way the incident was going to be used as an argument against Carnival. That simple, almost inadvertent gesture of putting a camera to the eye and taking a picture of one of the multitude of narratives that make up Carnival, was the one that would be given

primacy in the news that day and perhaps for the week or two that followed. It would not be the images of beauty, of artistic ingenuity, of mind-blowing organisational and logistical skills deployed by women, men and children over months in order to make the event happen. It would not be the capturing of the chance, sometime miraculous encounters between people that may blossom into lifelong relationships. It would be none of the things for which I had worked and studied in order to capture and portray as effectively as I could; but rather a photograph, perhaps badly exposed and taken almost as a reflex, of a white youth who got stabbed. And it really didn't matter if those who did it were also white. The fact was that it happened at Carnival.

I sat on that roll of film for a long time, in fact too long because, for some reason, it did me a favour of misplacing itself.

From time to time I find myself still searching for it. ▪

Angela Robinson Rangers Tropical Warriors

The first year we went on the road was actually the best year, because in carnival you don't know what to expect. The feeling you get when you see the crowd, hear the music, seeing everyone happy and carefree. I can't even describe that feeling.

1993 was the first year and everyone was enthusiastic about making the costumes. We tried them on during the dress rehearsal and it was amazing, everyone was pleased because they looked so colourful. It's quite a big troupe, and I think the bigger the troupe the better because everyone feeds off the adrenaline of the other members. It also looks better when you see this mass of colour on the road. The first year we participated we actually won for our costumes. Although we had very little money, we managed to make the headpieces and costumes. We wore plimsolls, which we decorated ourselves and we all held something in our hands. The troupe consists of members between the ages of two and forty, so you can imagine what that looks like with all the different age groups, different heights, etc.

Our procession in Leicester starts from Victoria Park, then goes down to Evington Road, which leads into St.Stephens Road, moves into Swan Street Bridge where there is a large West Indian population, allowing us to incorporate all these areas. Crowds follow us into the City Centre, where all the races, Chinese, White, etc., join us as we go back into the park on London Road.

The crowds get bigger and bigger as we go around until we get back to the park where the main stage and stalls are. After the procession, everything takes place on stage, the artistes perform and the costumes are judged. The stage is made for everyone to enjoy carnival especially those unable to follow the whole procession. That way the whole community gets a chance to take part in carnival.

Such colour! Such energy! Ah, the sound of enjoyment!
That smell! That smell? Yes the food of Carnival.
Just as the music, the food of Carnival brings out
our emotions and makes our senses prick up.
Take in a deep breath. You know you have arrived!

Richard Simpson
was born in Lewisham and has
been part of the borough's
community ever since.
He was a founder member of
Lewisham's first community
radio station, FIRST LOVE
(now FUSION 107.71 FM).
Married with six children, he is a
loved and respected family man.
As proprietor of CUMMIN UP,
a chain of Caribbean
take-aways and restaurants, he
is well aware of the interwoven
union of carnival and food.

Roti wrapped around goat, chicken or vegetarian curry - derived from the shores of Trinidad and Guyana.

Rice and peas, if your perspective is Jamaican, or peas and rice if it's not, has as many methods of production as there are cooks. You use red peas (kidney beans), black eye beans, cow peas, crab eye or gungo peas (pigeon peas). You use coconut cream for speed or grate the coconut and wash out the milk if you're not in any hurry. You add onions or escallion and pimento if you're a connoisseur and if your pot meets the test, you'll be able to eat it so-so (on it's own).

Curry anything! From lamb to fish and anything in-between. Goat curry for the meat eater is the festival dish. Carnival is the place for sampling. So much time and effort in the preparation! Seasoned at least a day ahead with lots of onion, garlic, hot scotch bonnet pepper and curry and then slow cooked, but devoured quickly with some white rice.

Pholourie, saltfish fritters or accra. What could they have in common? Well they are versions of a theme, made in a batter. The former you add jerra (cumin) and the latter you add fish to the flour, water, black pepper and onion base before frying. Both are lovely, on the move snacks, but don't forget the sauce or chutney to finish it up!

Pattie; there is the open Guyanese tart version or perhaps the better known Jamaican Pattie originally beef filled, but now there's a veggie, a lamb, a chicken, a saltfish, an ackee & saltfish, a calaloo & saltfish... You must try a few vendors to see " who is saying one" (the best!).

And there is roasting or barbecuing, reminiscent of the great, hot out door life of sea and sand. There is roast corn, plantain, sweet potato or yam, roast fish. But you will never be far from a jerk pit - the Jamaican speciality of heavily seasoned meat, extremely hot once the scotch bonnet peppers get a hold, then thrown on the coals.

Bakes, fried dumplings, jonny cakes or journey cakes, if we momentarily forget the evolutionary process that corrupted its name, by definition a bread. Yes, only flour, but the know how! Round crafted balls with a golden appearance, with

a slight crunch, thin skinned with a soft almost fluffy interior, no cracks, oil laden when the temperature of the frying oil is not hot enough, or dark and tuff when the oil is too hot… Yes, the know how! Certainly a treat on the move or a welcome accompaniment to a well-deserved side walk meal as you replenish your energy store.

Escoveitch fish, the colour of the garnish alone is a spectacle, goat fish, snapper fish, red bream or coley; first fried then left to marinate in vinegar immersing red & green sweet peppers, lime onions and pimento served with hard dough bread!

Just as you select your dancing partner the "borra" (round discs of pasty) needs the channa (chick peas) for the carnival sandwich, 'Doubles'. Served also with a hot chutney. Your feet will not be the only thing dancing, as your taste buds get excited with this simple Trini marvel.

As the evening progresses soup may be the thing for the Ital (vegan) palette. Any bean can start a good broth but there must be lots of spinners (snake looking dumplings), Yam, sweet potato, cassava and even pumpkin. This represents a well balanced meal and not necessarily heavy to continue to wine into the sunset.

For the vegetarian; stew peas (kidney beans) cooked in coconut milk with lots of 'Spinners', tiny dumplings that are torn from a lump of flour held in one hand towards the fingers whilst the palms roll it and then tossed into the bubbling pot rhythmically. Veggie

curry laden with carrots, chocho, Irish potato (to differentiate from the sweet potato) garnished with fresh coriander.

If you've had enough of rice or always wondered what sweet potato tastes like, you'll not have to go too far. Provisions like yam, boiled or roasted, green banana, cornmeal, boiled dumplings, even boiled plantain and if you search out the corners you may find some cassava. All of these will make an excellent accompaniment to any meal but if you have budgetary restraint then a little gravy over it will certainly fill one up fast!

Entering the spirit or freeing the spirit is what Carnival is all about, or how about getting the spirit into you. There's a thirst quencher every few yards. There are alcoholic and non-alcoholic varieties. Peanut punch - fresh milk, peanut butter, condensed sweet milk and mixed spice with a dash of vanilla. Exchanging the peanut butter for pineapple gives pineapple juice. Or the extracted juice from carrots for West Indian carrot juice. Sour sop, banana or mango pulp all provide an excellent drink. Then of course add spirit (normally rum) to taste! All of these punches have an ital version by substituting the milk with water, the condensed

milk with sugar and adding a twist of lime. Traditional "sorrel" will always be on hand - a drink made from the leaves of the Hibiscus flower that, as you might imagine has a deep red colour but is light and refreshing. Another is "mauby" made from the bark of the carob tree, which in itself is extremely bitter but is then sweetened and spiced up with some cinnamon or cloves. All bitter drinks are said to be good for toning the blood, but if your inner health is not paramount at this time the latter option may take a bit of getting used to! But the real thirst quencher for those who are intent on dancing the day away is traditional lemonade, just lemon juice water and sugar, a long glass and lots of ice! If you're out to disguise your bevy, then grab a rum punch. Any mix of fruit juice, lime water, sugar, syrup and of course, this

time plenty of rum but you'll still need a long glass and plenty of ice.

As there are delightful colour schemes and designs in Carnival, the same must be said for the confectionery, a welcome end to any street side meal to give an extra energy boost. Coconut drops - pieces of chopped coconut boiled in sugar with a hint of ginger, peanut cake substituting the coconut for peanuts. Pawpaw balls and tamarind balls, the flesh of the fruit boiled in sugar then formed in balls. Angel's food, simply segmented oranges with a sprinkling of coconut. If you have had your induction then try some cowfoot jelly! The gelatinous stock produced from the boiling of the cow foot when making the stew is strained, sugar added, of course rum, milk and strawberry syrup for colour, tastes far better than it sounds! Sweet

potato and cornmeal puddings are two, which are very deep-seated in tradition. There's also spiced bun served with cheese, plantain tarts and gizzarda, desiccated coconut boiled with sugar and spices in a pastry coat. To further demonstrate the diverse cultural mix and amalgamation, there is one which is as Afrikan as they come. Dokono Gemi Gemi or Blue Draws Cornmeal prepared in coconut milk, sugar, currants and cinnamon mixed and enveloped in a banana leaf, or in our case foil, then boiled. They come no better than that.

If fruits are your thing, you'll always find a sugar cane vendor on the corner, not only offering sugar cane but also water melon, mangoes, sweet sop as well as the more common banana, pineapple, oranges and possibly many others. ▪

Michael 'Speedy' Ramdeen　Mahogany Arts

In Trinidad, Carnival was the one time of the year where you would find all the different races coming together in harmony. The rest of the year my Indian friends would call me "Nigger", my Black friends would call me "Coolie". In between there was no happy medium until carnival time came around and all the Indians and Black people realising

my costume making skills always wanted me to make for them.

Carnival was the one time that the unity in the nation really came together and showed its face. I always wondered if there was some way I could promote carnival to the rest of the world and get that unity.

Mas, Music and the Media

Stephen
Spark

Why is the carnival we read about in the papers so often unrecognisable as the one we attend?

Stephen Spark grew up in the least bacchanalian of English counties, Surrey, but on moving to London quickly became infected by the carnival virus and dependent on regular supplies of soca tapes from friends in Trinidad. Stephen is a member of South Connections mas band. His experiences as writer, photographer and sub-editor at Soca News were expanded when writing his Journalism Studies MA dissertation on the press reporting of Notting Hill Carnival.

Some commentators have characterised it as a conspiracy by the press, in league with the police and state, to denigrate and marginalise the country's largest celebration of black culture. Some blame journalists' obsession with sensationalism at the expense of balance and truth. Others see the roots of the problem lying in racism, prejudice, fear and ignorance.

In the early years, Notting Hill Carnival attracted scant attention outside its immediate area; it was simply a local celebration. Yet, even before the event had grown to national stature, the news agenda had already been set. Notting Hill was associated in the minds of journalists and the public with the race riots of the 1950s, poverty, immigrants, overcrowding, and unrest between residents and police. When it came to reporting Carnival, the "pegs" journalists hung their stories on were those same themes of race, rioting, policing and overcrowding.

It was perhaps inevitable that when disorder broke out at Carnival in the 1970s, the journalists were ready with a formidable battery of attention-grabbing three- and four-letter words - riot, mob, thug, gang, stab and loot. Their effect was felt way beyond newspaper-buyers, for the two-inch-high bold headlines shouted the news on buses and trains and to anyone passing a news vendor's stall. The message was soon absorbed: Carnival was dangerous.

Newspapers are read and written in the context of the times and for news editors in the early 1980s that context was urban unrest. The miners' strike, the poll tax riots, and the sporadic uprisings in Brixton, Toxteth, St. Paul's, Tottenham and elsewhere gave new life to the Notting Hill disorder "peg". Riot was what made Carnival newsworthy and justified the coverage. It was the way by which journalists interpreted Carnival for their readers, a means of fitting it in to a pre-existing, easily understood category of news.

During the 1990s, the reporting of Notting Hill Carnival changed in tandem with the overall news context. By the turn of the century, urban crime, rather than civil unrest, dominated the news agenda, and Channel-hopping asylum-seekers had long taken over from Commonwealth immigrants as the tabloid headline-writer's target of choice. The event itself was transformed, moving out of its troubled adolescence into what seemed, by 1999, to be a settled adulthood. Companies and politicians alike began to recognise Carnival's promotional potential. In public relations terms it was sexy – to the soft-drink company, record promoter or wannabe London mayor, Notting Hill was the essence of Cool Britannia, the focal point for the UK's cutting-edge

urban/youth/multi-ethnic cultures. But then came 2000's two murders and, later, organisational upheavals, and suddenly it did not seem quite so cool to be associated with Carnival.

A survey of the language used in Carnival reports over the past 15 years provides a fascinating insight into this evolution. If we look at 1987, for example, the word-group that appeared in the largest number of reports was "police" (including, "policing", "PC", "WPC", "cop"), which was referred to in three-quarters of the articles reviewed. In second place, covered by half of all the reports, were "trouble" and "riot", plus the number of people attending the event and the number of crimes. "Crime", "criminals", "violence", "murder/killing/death", "stab/bing", "youth", number of arrests, "injury/wound", "rob/robbery", "steal", "[throw] bottles", "stewards" and "riot gear/shield" all receive mentions in more reports than "revellers", "dance/dancer" or "costume". Police officials were quoted in three-quarters of the articles, Carnival organisers in just over one-quarter, and mas band and steel band leaders and designers in only two articles.

Superficially, at least, newspaper reports of Notting Hill Carnival made happier reading in 1998. The number of people attending was the most popular reference for journalists, appearing in half the articles surveyed. Almost as many referred to it as a "major event" or "the biggest event of its kind/in Europe/in the world" - a news peg used without

fail by London's Evening Standard. Other popular words and concepts were "sponsor/ship", "float", "food and drink", "sound system", "reveller" and "dance". Some words, though, were more persistent: "police" was up there in second place, and police officials were and still are the most commonly quoted named individuals.

Words, though, tell only half the story, for the choice of pictures can be at least as important as the headline in announcing the editorial stance of the piece. Pre-Carnival articles generally make use of a limited range of pictorial stereotypes - ones that, in the view of the picture editor, most immediately say "Carnival" to the average reader. An attractive young black female masquerader in The Independent and a black policeman dancing with a young, black female carnival-goer wearing his helmet (Evening Standard) were two typical examples from 1987. In 1998 the Evening Standard and The Times each used the same Press Association (PA) photograph of a masquerader who was, of course, attractive, young, black and female.

After-event coverage from the two years differed considerably however. Prominent on the front page of the Evening Standard and The Star, and on page 3 of the Evening News is a night-time photograph of three policemen in riot gear standing over a young black man on the ground, his face contorted in pain. In the foreground a policeman, hand on truncheon, strides towards the camera, his face tense and

whitened by the flash from the camera. The picture, credited to Keith Pannell in The Star, summarises the press's perception and portrayal of Notting Hill Carnival in the 1980s. The image is starkly black and white; the harsh light of the flash gun allows for no grey areas. In the news context of the time, and in the specific context of headlines such as "mob fury" and "riot mob terror", this melodramatic photograph offers an instant reading of "trouble at Carnival", creating a link to a range of possibly unrelated social issues.

By contrast, 1998's illustrations simply carried on from the pre-event coverage - an identical PA photograph of smiling masqueraders in The Guardian and The Financial Times, for example, and the obligatory policeman (white, this time) dancing with a black female masquerader. In an echo of 1997's main news story on William Hague's (then leader of the Conservative party) attendance at Notting Hill Carnival, there were also photographs in The Independent and The Daily Mail of London mayoral contender Lord Archer posing with attractive, young white and black female masqueraders.

The more positive message put across in recent years ought to be a source of satisfaction to those of us who love Carnival. Yet there is still something profoundly unsatisfying about the majority of articles on Notting Hill Carnival. One set of clichés seems to have been replaced by another - softer-edged, for sure, but still managing to miss the point. This is Carnival seen through a murky glass and heard while wearing earplugs. Even the supposed eyewitness accounts read as if they have been written from information supplied at third-hand.

In this game of Chinese Whispers played in a hall of distorting mirrors, bizarre interpretations of unfamiliar words appear and wild guesswork has to stand in for facts. The writers appear to have been cast adrift with an unreliable and incomplete phrasebook among a people whose language they do not speak. Hence we have The Independent speaking of "massed bands" and the Evening Standard's music correspondent Tim Lusher describing how "the steel drums of the soca floats pounded out a hypnotic jangling beat". Few writers have grasped the difference between mas bands, steel bands, mobile (soca) sound systems or music trucks, and decorated floats, and still less the distinctions between steel pan music, soca, calypso, samba, reggae and the myriad musical genres played by the static sounds.

In this there is a clear continuity than between the 1980's and the present. Unlike classical music, theatre, reggae, jazz, cinema or gardening, Carnival is not served by knowledgeable writers in the national press who can pen informative, interesting and accurate articles on their subject. Overwhelmingly white and middle class, journalists on the national dailies struggle to understand an alien culture through the medium of the clippings file and the PA newsflash. Like wealthy residents of Ladbroke Grove snatching glimpses of the bacchanal from their balconies, they are outsiders looking down from a great height. Understandably, they interpret Carnival in ways they feel most comfortable with - as news (disorder, police statistics, visits from politicians), light relief (dancing policemen), human interest (cute children), problem (noise, residents' complaints), exotic (non-European cultures and customs) and white or mainstream music (which certainly does not include soca). Even the black weekly newspapers frequently struggle to compile balanced, accurate accounts of Carnival beyond the themes of fashion, food and Jamaican- or US-derived music.

Unlike the Edinburgh Festival, for example, Carnival lacks status as an arts event. Reviews of the mas to be seen on the streets of Notting Hill Carnival are limited to passing references to glitter, feathers, sequins and wings. The music either "blasts" or "blares" from "massive sound systems" or comes from the "beat of steel drums". Masqueraders are "smiling carnival dancers", the Notting Hill Carnival Trust collectively are the (usually unnamed) "organisers". No wonder the world of the mas bands is such a mystery to most carnival-goers. The event happens each year without reason, without explanation, created by faceless, voiceless people, who somehow conspire to create either "Europe's greatest street party" or "a mayhem of knives and broken bottles", depending on the pre-set news agenda of the year.

Journalists' deep-rooted lack of understanding of Carnival makes the event easy prey for predatory reporting. It is an annual event, a predictable photo opportunity for the national dailies. In mid-August the fat file of articles from previous years will be opened and the screaming headlines of the 70s and 80s noted once again. Notting Hill Carnival's schedule suits the daily papers, for it can be a useful space-filler over the quiet holiday period, the daytime generates attractive pictures, and there is always the chance of a dramatic hard news story developing at just the right time to catch the front page. Even in a year without drama, Carnival can provide a story, for the one certainty is that the Metropolitan Police will provide statistics on the number of crimes reported, the number of arrests, the number of police on duty and estimates of the size of attendance. Hospitals, the emergency services and local politicians can all be relied on to provide casualty figures or newsworthy quotes. The relationship between journalists and these institutional contacts is usually very close, involving mutual trust and respect. Sources contacted only rarely or never before, such as carnival organisers, mas band leaders and ordinary masqueraders, lack the all-important elements of familiarity and trust. As a result, these voices are muted or silent.

The unremitting pressure of deadlines, combined with tight budgets and reduced staffing levels, means that, contrary to popular perception, journalists research and write most stories from their desks. The raw material for newspapers arrives second-hand down the telephone or by fax or e-mail, from institutional sources, from public relations companies and from press news agencies such as the Press Association. There is rarely time to research stories in depth or to seek alternative points of view from individuals or groups who are hard to track down. The distortions and superficiality of much Carnival reporting is less the result of deliberate bias than of lack of time and inadequate access to informed sources.

In the absence of a knowledge base among journalists, Carnival needs a high-profile, reliable, unbiased voice able to speak authoritatively for the multitude of participants. It should be able to direct the media quickly to appropriate individuals such as designers, mas-makers, calypsonians, pannists or soca experts. Most critically it should be media-aware, feeding the press with stories that meet editors' criteria of newsworthiness, so that it is Carnival that sets the news agenda, not the police.

In the past, those responsible for running Carnival seem to have

lacked an understanding of the way the press operates. If the journalist is seen as an enemy and starved of facts, other, less friendly sources will be quick to fill the information vacuum. Deliberately frustrating the press is not, in the long term, a sensible tactic and is often self-defeating. For example, by the time the results of the Carnival competitions are reluctantly released, the Costume Gala, Calypso Monarch finals, Panorama and Carnival itself are no longer news. Yet these could so easily be the means by which the perceptions of both press and public are turned around, from Carnival as problem to Carnival as the cultural highlight of the year.

The language of newspapers' Carnival reporting may have changed over the past decade, but the underlying division between observers and observed is as strong as ever. The public is no better informed about the origins, development and artistry of the Carnival disciplines than it was 10 or 20 years ago. For most British people it is simply a big street party, an annual festival of drunkenness, Jamaican patties and reggae, enlivened by scantily clad women in sequins. To the thousands who give freely of their talents, energy and passion to create mas and music on the streets of west London each year, this is as belittling as characterising Carnival as a public-order problem.

Carnival deserves to be taken seriously as an artform in the UK. When we can read reports in the arts pages of the national dailies under the byline of "carnival arts correspondent" we will be able to say that Carnival in the UK has truly come of age. ▪

Joan Anim-Addo West Indian Broadcasting Service

As an island people we sang a lot. Still do. Visit Grenada at Christmas and you'll find endless singing. Men and women, boys and girls sing. Radio programmes reflect this. In the 1950's, the wireless was a key source of popular culture. Calypso was not so big but, like cricket, it figured in peoples' lives both locally and on the wireless. So, during the run up to Carnival, despite rebuke from the very many God fearing members of the community, we sang calypso. Of course, several of the songs were deemed unsuitable for children's ears. We heard snatches anyway and wondered why adults smirked or laughed openly or shook their heads at some of the lyrics. If the words couldn't be sung, it was still alright to hum the tunes and to shake your waist. The younger at heart tuned into the Windward Island Broadcasting Service, (WIBS) or, even better, the voice of Radio Guardian or Radio Trinidad so as to learn some of the hottest tunes on the neighbouring island. Sparrow, the calypsonian was not Mighty; was not yet on the scene but Kitchener was. In Grenada, he is remembered for his tour of the island as a young calypsonian. Like many aspiring young artists, he took an important step by visiting local schools and finding his first audiences there. The young people at that time still remember 'Chinee Never Have a VJ Day', social commentary that parents probably found more preferable to 'Kitch, Let's Go to Bed'.

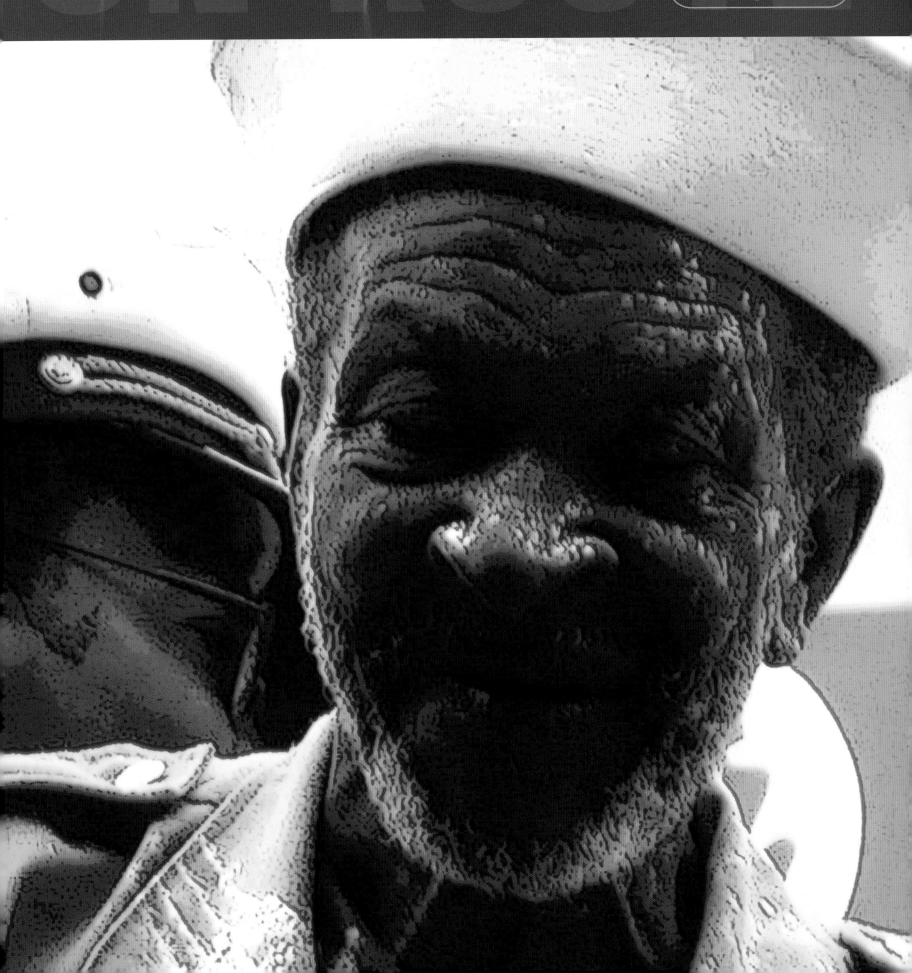

A Carnival Bibliography

A. Ruth
Tompsett

Where do today's carnivals in Britain come from? What do the masquerades mean? Who designs the stunning costumes? How are the pans made?

A. Ruth Tompsett is Principal Lecturer in Performing Arts at Middlesex University, London. In 1986 she introduced Carnival Studies to the BA Performing Arts programme and has since established a widely used archive and resource for carnival study at the University. She has lectured and run workshops on carnival in universities and arts projects in the UK, USA, South African and the Caribbean. in 1997, she organised 'Catch the Spirit: a Carnival Arts Conference' at Museum of London. Ruth is an adviser to London Arts.

Whether you have not yet been to carnival or have indeed been and enjoyed it or whether you have been born into the culture and play mas every year, if you are interested in studying carnival there is a range of published material to refer to.

In the process of identifying books that can be useful for learning about carnival, this chapter suggests approaches and topics that may fruitfully open up the whole area of carnival studies. Carnival itself is often controversial and the reader will find a rich mix of perspectives and material in the range of texts introduced below.

Carnival traditions exist in many parts of the world, rooted in festivals of regeneration. Celebrations and rituals involving masquerade belong in the history of societies across the globe. Many theatre companions and encyclopaedias will offer information on the nature and origins of carnival and masquerade traditions, though generally from a distinctly Western perspective. John Mack's **Masks, The Art of Expression**, offers soundly researched and accessible description of masquerade practices in many different societies, while Paul McLaren, in a short essay in Uschi Dresing's **Play Mas**, succinctly puts today's Caribbean-style carnivals into the context of older or parallel carnival and masquerade traditions.

Today's spectacular carnivals in Britain derive from Caribbean festival celebrations, most particularly from the Trinidad Carnival, and their development is inseparable from the political and social history of Britain and the Caribbean. To trace that history is to gain detailed insight on the nature and development of Caribbean Carnival and its significance in the diaspora. The **Insight Guide** on Trinidad offers a readable, and at the same time authoritative, starting point. More substantial are Eric Williams' **History of the People of Trinidad** and Bridget Brereton's **History of Modern Trinidad, 1783-1962**, while books that trace the intimate connection between historical events and carnival development include Fr. Anthony De Verteuil's **The Years of Revolt: Trinidad 1881-1888**, **Carnival, Canboulay and Calypso** by John Cowley and Hollis Liverpool's **Rituals of Power and Rebellion**.

For the origins of the still prevalent music forms of calypso, soca and pan, and of such masquerades as the stilted Moco Jumbie, the visually impressive Fancy Indian, Midnight Robber, sailor bands and many more, the seminal **The Trinidad Carnival** by Errol Hill is required reading. It is a rich and highly readable, well-indexed resource and reference. Peter Mason's **Bacchanal! The Carnival Culture of Trinidad** provides an overview of Trinidad Carnival's musics and mas,

looking forward as well as back, in a compact paperback, while the lavishly illustrated **Caribbean Festival Arts** by John Nunley and Judith Bettelheim provides insight on carnival arts together with the arts of comparative festivals throughout the Caribbean as well as in the diaspora. Two further publications, for academic study, are Peter van Koningsbruggen's thought-provoking **Trinidad Carnival, A Quest for National Identity** and **TDR's Special Issue** on Trinidad and Tobago Carnival which offers consideration of Trinidad Carnival today, in an historical context, and focuses on carnival's cultural diversity.

There are carnivals reflecting Caribbean influence in over thirty cities in Britain, of which the oldest and best known is London's Carnival at Notting Hill. Both Hill's new edition of **The Trinidad Carnival** and Nunley and Bettelheim's **Caribbean Festival Arts** offer discussion on Notting Hill Carnival and on carnival arts, while chapters in Kwesi Owusu's **The Struggle for Black Arts in Britain** and **Storms of the Heart** edited by Owusu, take the reader inside both the experience of carnival in London and its significance. The catalogue to the Arts Council's touring exhibition, **Masquerading: The Art of Notting Hill Carnival 1986** gives an authoritative and concise overview of the history and arts of Carnival at Notting Hill, together with Kwesi Owusu and Jacob Ross's **Behind the Masquerade: The Story of Notting Hill Carnival**. Access to photographs and illustrations are clearly crucial to anyone studying this area, and three of the publications cited here - by Nunley and Bettelheim, Owusu and Ross, and

Arts Council of Great Britain - include valuable photographic reference and illustration.

Some knowledge of the social and political history of post-war Britain will valuably contribute to understanding the meanings and significance of carnival and of its development here. The most substantial history of relevance is Peter Fryer's finely researched and very readable **Staying Power**, which starts with the Romans and brings us into the 1980s, while Mike Phillips and Trevor Phillips' **Windrush: The Irresistible Rise of Multi-Racial Britain** and Tony Sewell's **Keep on Moving: The Windrush Legacy** provide informative commentaries on post-war British history drawing significantly and tellingly on first-hand accounts and personal experience.

Carnival is party and art. It is also claiming of space, celebration and exploration of identity. Study of carnival's history and significance opens up questions about media treatment of carnival and issues of culture and identity. Useful resources in studying such aspects include Winston James and Clive Harris's **Inside Babylon**, specifically the chapter by Cecil Gutzmore, and Abner Cohen's **Masquerade Politics. The Art of Being Black** by Claire Alexander, while not specifically focussing on carnival, may be a useful source of more general reference in exploring black British culture and identity. Michael La Rose's **Mas in Notting Hill: Documents in the Struggle for a Representative Carnival** and **Police Carnival 1989**, provide invaluable insight on

the policing, press reporting and organisation of Notting Hill Carnival in more recent times.

The books by Hill, Nunley & Bettelheim, Owusu and Ross and the Arts Council Exhibition Catalogue each discuss the arts of mas and costume, variously examining specific examples, identifying key designers or tracing the process of costume-making in the mas camp and the playing of mas on the street. Peter Minshall's champter on carnival in **Caribbean Visions** closely examines the carnival artform.

At present there is no publication specifically focussed on the techniques used in costume-making, but **Engineers of the Imagination: The Welfare State Handbook** by Tony Coult and Baz Kershaw offers relevant guidance for making costumes for street performance. **Masquerade: Schemes of Work for Art in the Primary School**, by Cam, Elia and Lawlor is a rich source of ideas and approaches for practical study of carnival with children. The pack makes connections across a range of festivals, of which carnival is one, but the connections in themselves are enlightening and the wider range of reference is relevant to carnival art work. Both books have the advantage of presenting ideas and techniques that have been thoroughly tried and tested.

When costume bands select their themes for carnival they draw topics and ideas from nature, sci-fi, history, traditional mas, popular culture, science and literature. African heritage continues to be a significant source of inspiration and designers draw imaginatively on African art, history and masquerade traditions. Although it is difficult to trace Caribbean masquerades back to specific West African traditions there are many points of comparison to be made. Whether seeking ideas for costume design or to gain a richer understanding of the nature of masquerade, books can be an invaluable resource. **Africa: The Art of a Continent**, edited by Tom Phillips, **Black Africa: Masks, Sculptures, Jewellery**, by Laure Meyer and John Mack's book mentioned above offer both visual material and informative commentaries in large art book format. Frank Willet's **African Art**, in the Thames and Hudson World of Art series, gives an historical overview and challenging commentary, illustrated throughout, within a comparatively small and competitively priced volume. It is often said that the mask or artefact exhibited in a museum or presented on the page is only half the story. To understand the meaning of a mask it must be seen in action. Two books that can take a reader at least part of the way are **Africa Dances** by Michel Huet and Claude Savary and **Yoruba Ritual: Performers, Play, Agency** by Margaret Thompson Drewal. Drewal, a performance theorist, offers detailed description of the key rituals of Yoruba life, with useful black and white illustration. **Africa Dances** is a large art book, predominantly made up of Huet's colour photographs of dances and ceremonies. The photographs are remarkably immediate and communicative and provide a rich insight on the detail and nature of ritual performance,

including masquerading, from many parts of Africa.

In considering the visual heritage in Caribbean carnival and the diversity of influences on costume aesthetics, it is important to acknowledge also the impact of East Indian arts. The ancestors of the majority of today's Trinidadians came from either West Africa or the Indian subcontinent, predominantly from North and North-Eastern India and a smaller number from the South. The colours of Indian textiles and the reflective qualities of decorative materials such as sequins, mirror fragments and gold and silver thread have had a profound effect on costume design in Trinidad Carnival, particularly in the twentieth century, and in the Caribbean carnivals of the diaspora. Books on Indian arts may suggest, in general terms, how Caribbean carnival arts have been influenced in respect of colour ranges, materials and techniques. The many and detailed photographs in **The Performing Arts of Kerala** by M. Sarabhai, and Krishna and Rajamani's **The Arts and Crafts of Tamilnadu** are richly informing on Southern Indian traditions of floral art, cloth dyeing, body adornment and chariot decoration, to name but a few. It seems likely that the decorative arts from both Hindu and Muslim festivals in Trinidad have influenced the carnival aesthetic. In the Muslim commemorative event of Hosay, for example, elaborately constructed and highly decorative 'tadjas', replicas of domed tombs, together with two large ornamented moons are carried through the streets of Trinidadian towns. Craftsmen and technicians who work on both carnival costumes

and Hosay structures take techniques of building and decoration between the two. Nunley and Bettelheim's **Caribbean Festival Arts** includes an informing chapter on Hosay.

It is impossible to think of mas without thinking of music. Sound systems too offer reggae, rap and hiphop, not to mention soul, Rn'B, funk and jazz, drum and bass and jungle, house and garage, soca, calypso and zouk. Whatever the radio stations and music magazines are focussing on at that moment will be on the streets at carnival time and these are the best sources of information on these musics. The carnival programmes that come out during carnival time and the organiser's Official Programme usually contain articles and specific information on bands, artists and sound systems. Traditionally the musics of Caribbean Carnival are steel band, calypso and soca and these are most often to be heard on the music trucks that accompany the costume bands. Peter Manuel's **Caribbean Currents: Caribbean Music from Rumba to Reggae** is informative on calypso, soca and steel band, and also on other relevant musics such as salsa, reggae and ragga. Paul Oliver's **Black Music in Britain** offers an authoritative account of steel band development in Britain, while Cy Grant's valuably illustrated **Ring of Steel** puts pan in its Caribbean context as well taking in pan's development and influence globally. John La Rose's interview with the internationally renowned David Rudder, published by New Beacon Books, and the magazines **Soca News** and **Pan Podium** are

informing on contemporary music developments. Whilst the origins and history of calypso are detailedly and authoritatively explored in John Cowley's book, mentioned above, and Gordon Rohlehr's **Calypso and Society in Pre-Independence Trinidad**.

While many of the texts referred to so far are particularly valuable for historical and cultural study, an alternative approach to gaining an understanding of carnival would be to read works of the imagination. Poems, short stories and novels can initiate a reader into something of the spirit and meaning of carnival and none more so than Earl Lovelace's novel **The Dragon Can't Dance**. Short story collections such as those edited by Stewart Brown and Mervyn Morris contain stories about stick fighters, pan men, Papa Bois and Diablesse, aspiration and competition, playing dragon or being King of the band. Two poets particularly notable for their celebration of the mas and music of carnival are Grace Nichols and John Agard. Nichols' **Sunris**, in a volume of the same title, is a highly dramatic poem, in which all of carnival is vicariously experienced, while in his poem series in **Man to Pan** Agard evokes both the music of pan and the energy and ecstasy of playing it. For a magical and diverse collection of poems by different poets celebrating and evoking carnival turn to Brown, Morris and Rohlehr's **Voiceprint**, a classic collection of oral and related poetry from the Caribbean.

The greatest study of carnival is carnival itself. To sew, glue or weld in the mas camp where the costumes are made, to play mas on the street on carnival day or simply to be there moving with all that moves the body and spirit in carnival is to gain a knowledge that comes with being and doing, an inside knowledge that is second to none. If you're studying carnival, make time to play mas. ■

Christina Oree Beeraahar Sweet Combination

I originated from Trinidad, from Hindu parents who were very strict and never wanted us to take part in carnival, although I used to participate in the Diwali festival. I was a classically trained dancer, performing kathak. In 1963, I came to the UK, and it was my daughter who got me involved in carnival.

In 1979 when she was looking for a carnival queen for the organisation she had formed, Quintessence, she chose me. My costume was called, 'Bitter Sweet'. It was a pink hibiscus flower, and the 'bitterness' was a snake head piece above the hibiscus, because when hibiscus hedges grow quite large, snakes often hide themselves in them. That year I won outright.

In those days the contest was held at the Commonwealth Institute, and winning it was ecstasy. It was exciting going on stage and representing Quintessence, knowing that the entire crowd is focusing on you and cameras are flashing. It was lovely being dressed up differently from when I took part in Diwali. Everybody was focused on me, directly on me. It was wonderful. My daughter was so proud of me. And gaining the appreciation of the crowd, it made me more enthusiastic to continue with carnival.

Bibliography

Below are given the details of the publications referred to in this chapter.

Agard, John, **Man to Pan** (London: Pluto Press 1982)

Agard, John, **Mangoes and Bullets** (London: Pluto Press 1985)

Alexander, Claire, **The Art of Being Black** (Oxford: Clarendon Press 1996)

Arts Council of Great Britain, **Masquerading: The Art of Notting Hill Carnival**
(London: Arts Council of Great Britain 1986)

Ayo, Yvonne, **Africa** (London, New York & Stuttgart: Dorling Kindersley Eye Witness Guides 1995)

Brereton, Bridget, **History of Modern Trinidad, 1783-1962** (London: Heinemann Educational 1981)

Brown, Stewart, **Caribbean New Wave, Contemporary Short Stories** (London: Heinemann 1990)

Brown, Stewart, Morris, Mervyn and Rohlehr, Gordon,
Voiceprint: An Anthology of Oral and Related Poetry from the Caribbean (London: Longman 1989)

Cam, J., Elia, R. and Lawlor, T., **Masquerade: Schemes of Work for Art in the Primary School**
(London: The Visual Learning Unit 1998)

Cohen, Abner, **Masquerade Politics: Explorations in the Structure of Urban Cultural Movements**
(Oxford and Provenance: Berg 1993)

Coult, Tony and Kershaw, Baz. **Engineers of the Imagination: The Welfare State Handbook**
(London: Methuen 1990)

Cowley, John, **Carnival Canboulay and Calypso: Traditions in the Making**
(Cambridge: Cambridge University Press 1996, paperback 1999)

De Verteuil, Fr. Anthony, **The Years of Revolt, Trinidad 1881-1888**
(Trinidad: Paria Publishing Company Ltd. 1984)

Dresing, Uschi, **Play Mas, Carnival der Kulturen**
(Germany: Kerber Verlag 1997) NB:text part in English, part in German

Drewal, Margaret Thompson, **Yoruba Ritual: Performer, Play, Agency**
(Bloomington and Indianapolis: Indiana University Press 1992)

Finley, Carol, **The Art of African Masks: Exploring Cultural Traditions**
(Minneapolis: Lerner Publications Company 1999)

Fryer, Peter, **Staying Power: The History of Black People in Britain** (London: Pluto 1984)

Grant, Cy, **Ring of Steel: Pan, Sound and Symbol** (London: Macmillan 1998)

Hill, Errol, **The Trinidad Carnival: A Mandate for a National Theatre** (new edition, London: New Beacon Books 1997)

Huet, Michel, (photography) and Savary, Claude (text), **Africa Dances** (London: Thames and Hudson 1995)

Insight Guides, **Trinidad and Tobago** (London: APA Publications GmbH & Co. reprinted 1998)

James, Winston and Harris, Clive, **Inside Babylon: The Caribbean Diaspora in Britain** (London: Verso 1993)

Koningsbruggen, van Peter, **Trinidad Carnival: A Quest for National Identity** (London: Macmillan Education 1997)

Krishna, Nanditha and Rajamani, V.K. (phot.), **Arts and Crafts of Tamilnadu**
(Ahmedabad: Mapin Publishing Pvt. Ltd. 1992)

Bibliography

La Rose, Michael and Peoples War Carnival Band, **Mas in Notting Hill: Documents in the Struggle for a Representative and Democratic Carnival 1989/90** (London: New Beacon Books 1990)

La Rose, Michael, **Police Carnival 1989** (London: New Beacon Books 1989)

Liverpool, Hollis, **Rituals of Power and Rebellion: The Carnival Tradition in Trinidad and Tobago 1763-1962** (Chicago, USA: Research Associates School Times Publications 2001)

Lovelace, Earl, **The Dragon Can't Dance** (London: Longman 1979)

Mack, John, (ed.), **Masks: The Art of Expression** (London: British Museum Press reprinted 1998)

Manuel, Peter, **Caribbean Currents: Caribbean Music from Rumba to Reggae** (U.S.A. : Philadelphia Temple University Press, 1998)

Mason, Peter, **Bachanaal! The Carnival Culture of Trinidad** (Philadelphia Temple University Press 1998)

Meyer, Laure, **Black Africa: Masks, Sculptures, Jewellery** (Paris: Terrail 1992)

Morris, Mervyn, **Contemporary Caribbean Short Stories** (London: Faber and Faber 1990)

Nichols, Grace, **Sunris** (London: Virago 1996)

Nunley, John W., and Bettelheim, Judith, **Caribbean Festival Arts: Each and Every Bit of Difference** (Seattle: University of Washington Press 1988)

Oliver, Paul, (ed.), **Black Music in Britain: Essays on the Afro-Asian Contribution to Popular Music** (Buckingham, U.K.: Open University 1990)

Owusu, Kwesi, (ed.), **Storms of the Heart: An Anthology of Black Arts and Culture** (London: Camden Press 1988)

Owusu, Kwesi, **The Struggle for Black Arts in Britain** (London: Comedia 1986)

Owusu, Kwesi and Ross, Jacob, **Behind the Masquerade: The Story of Notting Hill Carnival** (London: Arts Media Group 1988)

Pan Podium Official Magazine of the British Association of Steelbands

Phillips, Mike and Phillips, Trevor, **Windrush: The Irresistible Rise of Multi-Racial Britain** (London, Harper Collins 1998)

Phillips, Tom, (ed.), **Africa: The Art of a Continent** (Munich & New YoVrk: Prestel 1995)

Minshall, Peter, '**Carnival and it's Place in Caribbean Culture and Art' in Caribbean Visions: Contemporary Painting and Sculpture**, ed. Nancy Eikel

Riggio, Milla C., 'Trinidad and Tobago Carnival', special issue of **TDR** Vol 42 Number 3, Fall 1998

Rohlehr, Gordon, **Calypso and Society in Pre-Independence Trinidad** (Port-of-Spain, Trinidad: self-published 1990)

Sarabhai, Mallika and Shah, Pankaj (photography), **Performing Arts of Kerala** (Ahmedabad: Mapin Publishing Pvt. Ltd 1994)

Sewell, Tony, **Keep on Moving: The Windrush Legacy** (London: Voice Enterprises 1998)

Smart, I I & Nehusi, K S K, **Ah Come Back Home: Perspectives on the Trinidad and Tobago Carnival** (Washington DC, USA and Port of Spain, Trinidad: Original World Press 2000)

Soca News: The Caribbean Music and Culture Magazine (London: Soca News Magazine)

Willet, Frank, **African Art** (London: Thames and Hudson first published 1971, reprinted 1991)

Williams, Eric, **History of the People of Trinidad and Tobago** (London: Andre Deutsch 1964)

The Tremendous Scope for Caribbean Style Carnival in the Curriculum

Pawlet Warner

Caribbean Style Carnival cuts right across the national curriculum and can be used in Maths, English, History, Geography and the Visual and Performing Arts.

Carnival has a history linked with the old colonial rule that allows room to explore aspects of history usually forgotten. It also takes you on a world tour in terms of geography because Carnival has its roots in four continents: Africa, Asia, Europe, North and South America. Calypso gives the opportunity for a creative approach to English language looking at rhyming couplets, verse etc. Masquerade allows a unique approach to science and maths working out the dimension and scale when making costume that consist of large structures. As an artform, Carnival has tremendous scope as it combines both the performing and visual arts in one of the largest participatory events in the world.

VISUAL ARTS
Painting
Drawing
Sculpture
Wire bending
Copper plating

ENGLISH LANGUAGE
Reading
Writing
Poetry
Literature
Drama

PERFORMING ARTS
Dance
Music
Drama

MATHS & SCIENCE
Physics
Geometry
Trigonometry

INDUSTRIAL ARTS
Woodwork
Metalwork
Electrics

GEOGRAPHICAL & SOCIAL ISSUES
Caribbean Basin
Migration
Anthropology

HISTORY
Emancipation
Slavery
African & Christian religions
Festivals in the Caribbean in the Middle Ages
European Middle Ages religions,
customs and drama

PLAYS
Ping Pong by Errol Hill
Man Better Man by Errol Hill
Ti-Jean and his Brothers by Derek Walcott
Charlatan by Derek Walcott
Moon on a Rainbow Shawl by Errol Hill
The Drum Maker by Kendell Hippolyte

This book could not have been written without the knowledge shared
and generous help received from many organisations and individuals.

Arts Council England would like to thank everyone for their support and encouragement.

ON ROUTE CONTRIBUTORS:

Dotun Adebayo	Alexander D. Great
Joan Anim Addo	Bro Linton & Ras Benji
Celia Burgess-Macey	Monica Rene
Geraldine Connor	Jacob Ross
Carlton Garcia	Richard Simpson
Alan Dix	Stephen Spark
Pepe Francis	A. Ruth Tompsett
Dr Frances Harding	Pawlett Warner
Daniel Holder	

ON ROUTE stories were collected in interview and transcribed by **Deborah Kong**.

The following people were interviewed:

Lloyd Blake Birmingham Carnival
Arthur France Leeds Carnival
David Grant Beeraahar Sweet Combination
Alex Herbert Leeds Carnival
Christina Oree Beeraahar Sweet Combination
H Patten
Michael 'Speedy' Ramdeen Mahogany Arts
Angela Robinson Rangers Tropical Warriors
Clary Salandy Mahogany Arts

ON ROUTE interviews were transcribed by **Kate Laird**.

ON ROUTE was edited by **Pax Nindi** Senior Carnival Officer, Arts Council England

Editorial Assistance was provided by **Simone Hewer** and **Colin Prescod**

ON ROUTE was designed by **k3 & kargan media**

Photographers include **Simon Corry**, **Omar El-Houni**, **Pax Nindi** and **Antonio Pagano**.